Routledge Re

An Introduction to
Educational Computing

In both education and training, teachers are faced with many and varied problems relating to their teaching and their students' learning. Educational technology, in its widest sense, provides teachers with methods and tools which, if properly used, can alleviate some of these problems. The computer is one such tool, offering, within certain limitations, some possible solutions.

Originally published in 1979, this book describes the use of the computer as a resource and as a manager in education and training. It discusses the use, potential and limitations of this technology in helping the teacher and trainer.

Beginning with a consideration of the role of the computer as a mediator in the flow of information between the student and his learning environment, the book goes on to look at Computer Assisted Learning from an educational viewpoint, the strength and weaknesses of a number of different media, and the problems of managing modular courses and course structures and handling information on students' performance and progress.

A chapter on informatics and education addresses the problem of what both teachers and students should know about computers, while the final chapter examines the practical problems of prompting and organising the appropriate use of this technology.

From the author:

The use of information and communications technologies has moved on significantly since this book was published in 1979 – forty years ago – at a time when none of our current generation of learners and many of their teachers were yet born. The technology now is smaller, cheaper and more pervasive, and one of the consequences is that we see and use it in a very different context. So, at first sight, references to specific equipment (for example, graphics terminals) seem very antiquated. Fortunately, there are no images of the equipment used in the 1970s to astound the reader of the 21st century!

Yet, re-reading the book, I am reminded that many of the issues that faced the technology-based learning community then still face us now. Human evolution progresses slowly and the psychology of how we learn has not changed in the last forty years, although we may have a better understanding of the underpinning theory. Similarly, we seem little better at bringing about change in education and training systems: despite well publicised successes the long-awaited revolution that would automate our classrooms is still tantalizingly beyond our grasp. Indeed, there is still an unacceptable number of people worldwide who have little or no access to education – with or without technology.

We can trace the antecedents of educational computing far further back than the 1970s and there is no doubt that its development – under whatever name we chose to give it – will stretch far into the future. So, consider this book as a snapshot of the state of the art in 1979 and ponder on the changes that have happened since.

An Introduction to Educational Computing

Nicholas John Rushby

Routledge
Taylor & Francis Group

First published in 1979
by Croom Helm

This edition first published in 2019 by Routledge
2 Park Square, Milton Park, Abingdon, Oxon OX14 4RN

and by Routledge
52 Vanderbilt Avenue, New York, NY 10017

Routledge is an imprint of the Taylor & Francis Group, an informa business

Publisher's Note
The publisher has gone to great lengths to ensure the quality of this reprint but points out that some imperfections in the original copies may be apparent.

Disclaimer
The publisher has made every effort to trace copyright holders and welcomes correspondence from those they have been unable to contact.

A Library of Congress record exists under ISBN: 0856648132

ISBN: 978-0-367-26099-6 (hbk)
ISBN: 978-0-429-29148-7 (ebk)
ISBN: 978-0-367-26107-8 (pbk)

AN INTRODUCTION TO EDUCATIONAL COMPUTING

NICHOLAS JOHN RUSHBY

CROOM HELM LONDON

© 1979 Nicholas John Rushby
Croom Helm Ltd, 2-10 St John's Road, London SW11

British Library Cataloguing in Publication Data

Rushby, Nicholas John
    An introduction to educational computing.
    1. Computer assisted instruction
    I. Title
    371.39'445   LB1028.5

    ISBN 0-85664-813-2

CONTENTS

Acknowledgements

Preface 9
The Rationale for Educational Computing 9; The Intended Readership 9; An Overview of the Book 10

1. Introduction 12
Computers in Education and Training 12; The Uses of Computers in Education and Training 12; Some Problems of Education and Training 12; Differences in Aims and Methods between Education and Training 13; The Student and his Learning Environment 14; A Model of the Information Flow in Learning 15; Distinctions between CAL, CML and Student Record Systems 17; Justifications for Educational Computing 18; CAL as a Means of Saving Time and Resources 19; CAL as a Means of Improving the Quality of Learning 19; The Appropriate Use of CAL and CML 20

2. Computer Assisted Learning 22
Four Kinds of CAL 22; The Instructional Form of CAL 22; The Instructional Dialogue 23; Identifying the Student's Responses 24; Drill and Practice CAL 27; The Revelatory Form of CAL 27; Simulations in Nuclear Engineering, Statistics, Genetics and Medicine 28; Some Problems of Simulations 30; The Conjectural Form of CAL 31; Model Building, Hypothesis Forming and Testing 31; Modelling in Physics, Geometry and History 32; The Emancipatory Form of CAL 33; Serendipity Learning 34; The Rationale for CAL 36

3. Using Computer Assisted Learning 37
CAL and Other Media 37; Print Media 38; Tape Slide 38; Video 38; Lecturers, Tutors and Instructors 39; The Computer as Medium 40; The Multimedia Package 40; Producing CAL Packages 41; Presenting CAL Packages on Different Kinds of Terminals 41; Interactive or Batch Presentation 45; Single Students or Pairs of Students and CAL 45; Structuring the Material 47; The CAL Production Team 47; Package Documentation 49; Evaluation of the Package 50

4. Computer Managed Learning 52

The Rationale for CML 52; The CML Cycle 52; Assessment 53; Multiple Choice Tests 56; Computer Aided Marking 57; Feedback 60; Test Analysis 61; Analysis of the Test as a Whole 61; Analysis of Individual Questions 63; Item Banking and Test Construction 64; Storing Questions in the Computer 64; Using the Computer to Build Tests 67; Guiding Students through Structured Course Material 68; Record Keeping 69; Problems of Privacy 69; Reporting on Students' Performance and Progress 70; Reporting on Course Performance 71; Integrating CAL and CML 71; Linking CML to Library Circulation Systems 71; Student Record Systems 72; Careers Counselling 72; The Impact of CML on Education and Training 73; Resource Management 74; Computer Assisted Timetabling and Scheduling 74; Inventory and Stock Control 75

5. Informatics and Education 76

The Development of the Computer Specialist 76; Computer Awareness 77; Controlling how Computers Process Information 79; Living with Computers and their Effect on Everyday Life 80; A Methodology for Solving Problems 81; The Development of Problem-Solving Skills 82; An Informatics Methodology for CAL 82

6. Technological Aspects 85

The Computers 85; The Centralised Computer Centre 85; Dedicated Computer Facilities 86; Computing Facilities in Industry 87; Communications between the Computer and the Terminals 87; The Terminals 88; Alphameric Printing Terminals and VDUs 88; Graphics Terminals 89; Special Purpose CAL Terminals 89; Interactive or Batch Computing 89; The Programs 91; General Purpose Programming languages 91; Special CAL Author Languages 91; Reliability and Resilience 92; The Costs of Educational Computing 93; The Costs of the Packages 94; The Costs of the Computers 94; The Costs of the Terminals 95; Cost-Effectiveness 96

7. Managing the CAL Innovation 98

Political and Social Pressures on Education 98; Co-ordinated National CAL Projects in Western Europe 100; Institutional Pressures on the Innovation 101; Technological Pressures 101; Three Different Kinds of CAL Project 101; Subject Based Projects 101; Institutional Projects 102; CAL Exchange Projects 103; Promoting CAL 103; The First Steps in Using CAL 104; Royalties and Credit for CAL authors

104; Introducing CML 105; A Model for Managing the CAL Innovation 106; Proposals for Developing CAL in an Institution 106

Bibliography 108

Glossary 113

Index 121

NEW PATTERNS OF LEARNING

The Purpose of this Series

This series of books is intended to provide readable introductions to trends and areas of current thinking in education. Each book will be of interest to all educators, trainers and administrators responsible for the implementation of educational policies and programmes in higher, further and continuing education.

The books are designed for easy access of information. Each contains a glossary of important terms in the subject and has an annotated bibliography of key works to enable the reader to pursue selected areas in depth should he or she so wish.

This, the first book in the series, is written by Nicholas Rushby of the Imperial College Computer Centre, London where he directs a project concerned with the use of computers in education as a resource. Until last year he co-ordinated a major project as part of the National Development Programme in Computer Assisted Learning.

Titles of other books in the series that will be available shortly are given on the inside back cover of this book.

Currently available is the second title in this series *Preparing Educational Materials* by Duncan Harris of the University of Bath.

P. J. Hills.
Guildford, 1979

ACKNOWLEDGEMENTS

It would be difficult to compile a list of all those people who have contributed, directly or indirectly, to the writing of this book, for such a list would include the names of everyone I have worked with for the last eight years and many more whom I have met or whose work I have studied. I have tried in this book to portray all the facets of the subject, the disadvantages and the limitations of computer assisted learning as well as its benefits and possibilities. Inevitably in doing so, my own views have been influenced by others. I have also called on some of the scepticism of its critics.

However, some friends and colleagues deserve special mention — Edward James, my longtime mentor who first aroused my interest in the subject, Richard Hooper who was the Director of the UK National Development Programme in Computer Assisted Learning, all our colleagues in the many educational and training institutions working in CAL projects under the aegis of the National Programme, and staff from CAL projects in Europe, particularly in France, Holland and Germany. To all these people I owe my thanks for their time and patience. The responsibility for my perceptions — and my possible misconceptions — of their work lies of course with myself.

Finally it is customary, and in this case very appropriate, to record my thanks to my wife and family for their tolerance. Writing the book has not been easy — least of all for them.

Nick Rushby

PREFACE

In both education and training, teachers are faced with many and varied problems relating to their teaching and their students' learning. Highly structured courses to meet the particular needs of individual students pose problems of instruction; modular course structures with more sophisticated assessment methods pose problems of student management; student centred courses pose problems of resource management; necessary practical experience may be time-consuming, expensive or impossibly dangerous. Educational technology, in its widest sense, provides teachers with methods and tools which, properly applied, can alleviate some of these problems. The computer is one of these tools, offering some possible solutions — but with some limitations too.

This book is concerned primarily with the use of the computer as a resource and as a manager in education and training; in other words, teaching with computers, rather than teaching about computers. However, as we shall see later, it is often difficult to distinguish between these two activities. Inevitably the use of computers in the teaching process helps the student to appreciate their capabilities and to dispel the aura of mystique which surrounds them. Further, it is very difficult to teach students about computers without using the computer itself.

The text has been written for practising teachers in all kinds of education and training environments, for students of education, and for administrators responsible for the implementation of educational and training policies and programmes. It is primarily a book about the potential and the use of a technology to help the teacher and trainer, rather than about the technology itself. Certainly, although it assumes some preknowledge about education, training, and the ways in which we teach and learn, it does not presume that the reader knows any more about computers than that these machines exist.

To avoid verbosity, the term education has been used in the text to mean training as well as education at all levels. Similarly, the word student should be taken to mean pupil, student or trainee, while lecturers, tutors and instructors are referred to collectively as teachers. Finally, as is customary, masculine pronouns have been used throughout; the avoidance of words like she and her is an attempt at brevity rather than an assumption that there are no women students, pupils, lecturers, tutors, teachers, trainees or instructors in education or training.

An Overview

It is important to realise that an in-depth knowledge of computers and their operation is not an essential prerequisite for using them to assist in teaching and training. There seems no good reason why a teacher should know any more about computers than about any other machine that he uses in his teaching, for example an overhead projector. Success in using an overhead projector depends on the way it is used and on the quality and relevance of the graphics rather than on an understanding of its design. The role of the computer as a mediator in the flow of information between the student and his learning environment is discussed in the first chapter, on education and information. A model based on the different kinds of information flowing in the learning process provides a means of describing, if not defining, the differences between computer assisted and computer managed learning.

Chapter 2 looks at 'Computer Assisted Learning' (CAL) from an educational viewpoint and examines four broad areas of use. In the first form, which owes its origins to the techniques of programmed learning, the computer is used to provide a tutorial dialogue in which the student is systematically led through the course. The focus of attention is on the subject material which the student must master. In the second form, it is the student who is the central feature and the computer is used to provide information about a particular situation or simulated system so that the student can explore it and learn about it. The third form of CAL supports the student while he forms and tests control of the learning process, sometimes devising his own models and programming the computer accordingly. The fourth area is concerned with reducing the unnecessary labour of learning by helping the student to carry out tedious calculations or extracting relevant information from large quantities of data.

Computer assisted learning is one, but only one, of the tools that the teacher can use in his teaching. Certainly it is a very charismatic tool, but to be effective it must be applied appropriately. Chapter 3, on 'Using Computer Assisted Learning', considers the strengths and weaknesses of a number of different media: books, tape slide, educational television, computer assisted learning — and live teachers too. This leads to the idea of a learning package, which consists of one or more contributions to a specific subject topic using a number of different media. One of these may be a CAL program.

The problems of managing modular courses and course structures, and handling information on students' performance and progress are covered in Chapter 4 on 'Computer Managed Learning' (CML). The length of this chapter reflects the extensive nature of the facilities that can be provided by a CML system. While CAL concentrates on the student and his learning, CML is concerned with helping the teacher and the student by relieving them of some of the routine, time-consuming management processes. These include the tasks of assessment, test analysis and item banking, guiding students through modular courses and beyond into their choice of career, the maintenance of student records with the attendant problems of privacy and accuracy, and reporting on the performance of students, the assessment methods and the course, to the students, their teachers and the education or training management. The chapter concludes with a brief description of the administrative applications of the computer in education and training, particularly for timetabling and resource management.

Chapter 5, on 'Informatics and Education', addresses the problem of what we should teach our students, and know ourselves, about computers. Should we teach our students how the computer operates and how to program it, or concentrate on its impact on society, its possibilities and limitations. In addition to the obvious link that the use of the computer in CAL and CML breeds familiarity rather than fear, there is a second connection, because part of the study of computing concerns a systematic approach to problem solving which can often be successfully applied to the problems of education and the educated.

To be effective, CAL and CML must be used appropriately. To be practicable, the technological and educational resources required must also be deployed appropriately. Educational computing brings together three interrelated kinds of resources: the provision of computing machinery, the development of computer programs, and the production of educational materials. Chapter 6, 'Technological Aspects', considers the cost of providing the technological resources and how this may be reduced.

The final chapter, 'Managing the CAL Innovation', examines the problems of promoting and organising the appropriate use of this technology in a number of institutions in different national educational systems. It discusses ways of managing the production of educational course material and the supporting computer programs, and the factors influencing and inhibiting the innovation.

Other books, papers and reports referenced within the text are included in an annotated bibliography of key works in educational computing. The final section of the book is a glossary which gives brief definitions of key terms in educational computing and in computing itself.

1 INTRODUCTION

Computers in Education and Training

The use of computers in education and training has been greatly influenced by the history of their introduction into universities, colleges
and industry, and by their use in applications other than education and
training. Many of the earliest recognisable computers were developed
and operated in universities on both sides of the Atlantic. Since those
early days, the computer has grown in importance as a research tool so
that now it would be unthinkable, in many subject areas, to carry out
research work without access to a computer. Next, the effective, large-
scale use of computers requires a cadre of trained staff to design and
support computing systems and to help potential users who may not be
skilled programmers. Teaching people about computers uses a substantial
amount of computer time and, traditionally, research and teaching
computing together account for most of the computing activities in
higher education. At secondary level, where the research aspect is absent,
computer education is dominant.

More recently, first in North America and then in Europe and elsewhere, teachers have realised that the power of the computer as a
machine for storing, organising and processing information can be
applied to teaching and learning. The computer may be used as a
classroom resource, as a calculator, as a model of some real-life situation
or as a means of producing animated visual aids. Alternatively it may be
used in the background to help with the classroom management, keeping
records of the students' performance and carrying out other supportive
functions.

In industry and commerce, the original reasons for installing computers were to support the every-day processes of the organisations; to
carry out the calculations for payroll and invoicing, to process stock
control information, to model the financial behaviour of the company
and its environment, to control production lines and processes, and
recently for more sophisticated applications such as airline reservation
and operating systems. As teachers came to realise that computers
could be used to support their teaching, so their colleagues in industrial
training saw that the computers already in their organisations could be
used to help in the training process.

Whether in education or training, teachers are faced with many and
varied problems relating to their teaching and their students' learning.

Highly structured courses to meet the particular needs of individual students pose problems of instruction; modular course structures with more sophisticated assessment methods pose problems of student management; student centred courses to meet the particular needs of individual students pose problems of resource management; necessary practical experience may be time-consuming, expensive, or impossibly dangerous. Educational technology, in its widest sense, provides teachers with methods and tools which, properly applied, can alleviate some of these problems. The computer is one of these tools.

Education and Training Systems

Education and training involve complex systems which concern students, teachers and parents, resources such as schools and colleges, educational or training administrators, society and industry. This system is subject to pressures from a number of sources. In particular, three pressures, political, technological and social, can be seen as exerting considerable influence on it. These pressures are discussed in more detail in Chapter 7.

In discussing the use of computing in all levels of education and in training, we must recognise that there are both significant differences between the two, and also common problem areas to which this technology may bring common solutions. These distinctions are perceived in different ways, by the practitioners who think in terms of outcomes, and by the educational or training technologists who think of the processes needed to achieve those outcomes.

One difference which is seen as significant by many teachers and instructors is that, while the main aim of the educational process is to benefit the student, in training it is the organisation that hopes to benefit by acquiring a more skilled person. The managers of educational and training systems have different expectations of their students' success. The aim of the training process is to ensure that as many as possible of the students achieve all the course objectives and hence complete the training successfully. Most education systems, by accident or design, operate by a process of periodic culling, so that only the most successful students at the end of each stage may pass on to the next.

The process of education tends to focus on the student as someone to be guided through his learning and encouraged to widen his aspirations so that he can fulfil his potential in society. Education is perceived by its participants as a democratic process while training, in contrast, is usually more prescriptive. Training tends to concentrate on the student's learning of the subject matter so that he acquires the necessary abilities and skill to carry out his role in the organisation. Clearly this is an oversimplification, because many training courses encourage students to extend their learning beyond mastery of the specified objectives, while much of education, particularly at the primary and secondary level, is concerned with the teaching of basic skills, such as arithmetic, and thus by the above definition is really training.

This difference in approach is also seen in the methods which are used to assess the students' performance and progress. Training commonly uses criterion-referenced testing[†] which seeks to establish whether the student has achieved specified objectives. Assessment in education has also a qualitative flavour, and examines not only whether the objectives have been mastered, but also the degree of excellence achieved and how well each student has performed by comparison with his peers.

There are also considerable differences between the aims and processes of education at different levels. The shift in emphasis away from skills training to more abstract forms of knowledge in secondary and higher education is one obvious difference. A less apparent distinction is the change in the locus of control of learning as the student matures and moves from secondary to higher education. For the first part of his formal education, the student expects to be told what he must do in order to learn. Later, it may be desirable to wean him from this dependence on his mentor so that he can learn to learn by himself and, hence, continue to learn effectively after the end of his formal education.

Behind these different teaching and learning methods and objectives lie the common problem areas listed earlier: problems of individualising instruction to meet the particular needs of particular students; problems of managing students and resources; problems of providing particular learning experiences. For these problems computer assisted and computer managed learning offer some possible solutions — but have some limitations too.

Students and Information

The milieu of educational computing abounds with Lewis Carroll-like phrases which authors use to mean just what they want them to mean, nothing more and nothing less. The literature is confused with near synonyms such as computer aided instruction and computer aided learning[†] which are sometimes used interchangeably, but for some authors have subtle differences of meaning. Certainly there is a difference between the processes of learning and instruction; instruction is not a necessary condition, and is seldom a sufficient condition, for learning.

[†]Words or phrases marked with a dagger are to be found in the Glossary at the end of the book.

The difference between computer assisted learning (or CAL)[†] and computer managed learning[†] (or CML) is more significant but difficult to define. Traditionally, the distinction has been that in computer assisted learning the learning material is presented to the student through the computer, while in computer managed learning the computer is used to direct the student from one part of the course to another and the learning materials themselves are not kept in the machine. So in CAL the student receives some detailed tuition from the computer whereas with CML he and his tutor get information about his performance and progress. However, many CAL systems also carry out some management functions. Similarly, some CML systems present tutorial information which would usually be associated with computer assisted learning. The difference between the two is therefore somewhat blurred.

In a simplistic view of the learning process, the student acquires knowledge by receiving information from his surroundings and organising it so that he can then retrieve specific items, make generalisations and extrapolations. The speed, and perhaps the quality, of some learning may be improved if the student works with structured learning materials and is given some individual guidance by his mentor on his selection of a route through the modules. This implies that the student will supply information about his progress, problems and preferences. Hence there is a two-way flow of information with facts and guidance coming from the environment to the student, and feedback coming from the student. This is illustrated in Figure 1.1.

Clearly this is but a crude and oversimplified model of the very complex processes which constitute learning; processes which we do not fully comprehend. It can be argued that until we have developed a better understanding of the learning process it is difficult to advance our use of educational technology. Perhaps — but then there are many teachers who are able to help their students to learn although they too lack a clear and complete theory of learning and it seems reasonable that we should proceed cautiously in advance of the theory.

This pragmatic view provides a convenient description of the various types of educational computing. The computer can be seen as a mediator of the two-way flow of information between the student and his learning environment. We have seen that there are various kinds of information, facts, feedback and guidance. There are also quantitative and qualitative differences in the information, depending on the scale at which the learning is examined. At the micro level, for example when the student is working in a small seminar group or is reading a book, the information is highly detailed and changes very rapidly. It is difficult to

Figure 1.1: The Student in His Learning Environment

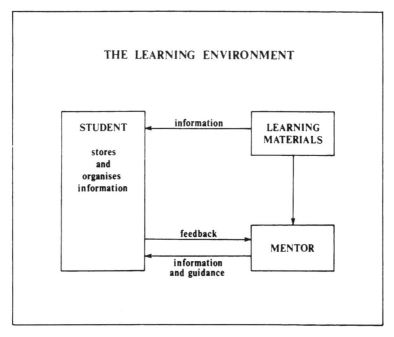

record and store all the information which is passed around during a lively discussion seminar, yet this is only a small part of each student's learning activities during a course which lasts for several weeks, months or years. In the longer term, this level of detail is unnecessary and a summary of the flow is more relevant. So there is another scale at which the learning process can be viewed, where the information is rather less detailed and changes less rapidly. This might be at the level where the student's activities are seen in terms of modules which take perhaps two or three hours to complete. Progressing further, this information can again be summarised to provide details of the learning process on a timescale which spans months, terms or years. Again there is less detail and a slower rate of change of information. This range of information detail and change is shown in Figure 1.2.

We should remember that the basic information considered in the model is the same throughout the range; it is the level of detail that is changing. At each stage the information is summarised and so reduced in quantity before being passed onto the next stage. So at the detailed end of the range there is a vast amount of information relating to each

Figure 1.2: The Spectrum of Educational Information

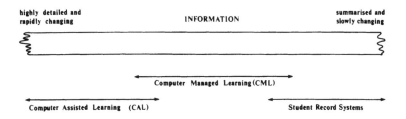

of the courses or course fragments which the student is using. As the information is summarised, individual fragments are combined to build a more complete picture of his studies. Deliberately, there are no boundaries shown between the separate stages because no real boundaries exist — each stage merges into the next. In considering the learning process, the student and his tutor will use an appropriate level of detail which will depend on the individual student and his course.

The different applications of computers to the learning process can now be described in terms of the way in which they mediate in the flow of information and of the levels of detail with which they are concerned. Thus, Computer Assisted Learning (CAL)[†] systems are involved with rapidly changing, highly detailed information and appear on the left hand side of the range. Computer Managed Learning (CML)[†] systems operate with less detailed information towards the middle of the range. Student record[†] systems appear on the right hand side and are concerned only with highly summarised accounts of the students' activities and results. These three descriptions are used as working definitions in this book. The term educational computing is used to cover the entire spectrum and also to embrace some other applications, such as computer assisted media production, which do not conveniently fit into the framework.

Lest it should seem that the definition of these terms is unduly belaboured, we should note that the confusion in the terminology of different authors has been the source of many misunderstandings and misconceptions by their readers. Some authors use these same names with small changes in emphasis, or different names with essentially the same meanings. Thus, particularly in North America and continental Europe, the terms 'computer assisted instruction'[†] and 'computer aided instruction' (CAI) are used to describe CAL. In the UK however,

CAI can imply an application in which the computer is used to administer drill and practice examples or programmed instruction; CAL is, in some way, a more sophisticated use of the computer. Elsewhere in the literature, CAL is taken to encompass the whole of the educational computing.[†] The descriptions 'computer based learning'[†] and 'computer based education'[†] (CBL and CBE) are also found as alternatives to educational computing.

Justifications

The introduction of computer assisted and computer managed learning in different institutions at different times may be ascribed to a variety of reasons, some of which are altruistic, some more selfish. Three objectives are often advanced in support of the innovation. It is said that CAL will provide:

 — savings in costs and resources,
 — more effective education or training,
 — intellectual challenge.

Firstly, it may be claimed that the new techniques will save time or effort, or both, and hence will either save the institution money, or enable the available staff to teach or train more students. Secondly, other things remaining equal, the same staff with the assistance of the computer can improve the quality of their teaching and their students' learning. A third reason is that the innovation will provide an intellectual challenge to the teachers with possibilities for evaluating courses more thoroughly and providing opportunities for a critical appraisal of their students' learning. A final incentive, infrequently expressed, is that CAL and CML are stimulating and charismatic; participants in this new area acquire an enhanced professional reputation. While the novelty of most innovations holds considerable appeal, this effect is particularly apparent where computers are concerned. Many people find programming and the mechanics of computing irresistibly attractive; some may even get addicted, as if to a drug, and exhibit withdrawal symptoms if they are separated from their computer. This may present a humorous picture, but it does pose a severe problem because the enthusiast's interest in the computer may obscure his judgement of its worth in a particular application. As we will see later, there is no good reason why a teacher must learn to write computer programs in order to use CAL. We should beware of forgetting our educational aims in the computing fervour.

As with many other educational innovations, although the justifications for developing CAL and CML have been educational, the decisions to experiment with educational computing and to develop and implement working systems have usually been taken for hard political and financial reasons. Following an initial stimulus, either from within the educational system or from outside it, politicians at a local or national level respond by making some funds available.

Savings in Time and Effort

The early development of computer assisted instruction in North America, and later in Europe and the Soviet Union, was largely in response to unfavourable staff-student ratios. The number of students rose rapidly and was not matched by an increase in the number of staff available to teach them. Any technology which would enable teachers to handle more students was worthy of investigation. Particularly in North America and the Soviet Union there was considerable interest in programmed instruction which offered many advantages, but also posed its own problems of controlling delivery, checking the students' understanding at each step and general management of learning. Computer assisted instruction was seen as an educational prosthetic which could extend the ability of the teacher to control learning and also extend his effective range. Programmed learning required the student to progress through mastery of small steps; if this technique was automated then the computer could not only hold the instructional material but could print it out on a typewriter for the student, check his ability to understand each step, and keep records of his progress. Because the load on the teacher was reduced, the staff-student ratio was effectively improved. The computer was used for drill and practice, for delivering programmed instruction and for keeping records of students' performance and progress. Thus the classical CAI and CMI (computer aided instruction and computer managed instruction) were developed and educational computing was linked in many teachers' minds with programmed instruction. The potential of educational computing is, of course, far greater than just the automation of programmed instruction, but this traditional misconception has proved very durable. Although the early aspirations of low-cost tutorial CAL[†] have still not been fully realised, the claim that CAL can save time and money is still used as a justification for many projects. The relative costs of teaching with computers and teaching by more conventional methods are discussed in Chapter 6.

Improving the Effectiveness of Learning

The early view of the computer as a machine which could help the available teaching staff to deal with greater numbers of students is now changing to a realisation that the technology, properly applied, offers the possibility of improving the quality of learning. Thus the cost-effectiveness of education and training is improved, but due to greater effectiveness of learning rather than by a reduction in costs. For example, practical experiments which may be impossibly dangerous, costly or time-consuming, can be simulated on the computer; highly individualised student centred courses which require considerable resources to operate can be viable if the functions of assessment, guidance, record-keeping and reporting are supported by a computer managed learning system; the computer can be used to retrieve and process information so that the student can explore existing knowledge and create new knowledge. The quality of learning can be improved directly by tailoring the course to the needs of individual students, for example by providing learning opportunities which would otherwise be impractical. There are also some indirect benefits, because educational computing demands a systematic approach to teaching and may force teachers to re-examine their existing methods and materials. This critical appraisal of the existing system may, independently of the computer, lead to substantial improvements.

Using the Computer Appropriately

The original hopes that educational computing could provide improved, individualised education at low cost were unrealistic and led to widespread disenchantment with the technology. Our expectations of qualitative improvements have been fulfilled in many cases, but there are still a number of pitfalls which must be avoided. The purpose of educational computing is to assist in the teaching and learning process, rather than to find an application for computing. The technology must be the servant and not the master. There are some educational problems for which the computer is an appropriate solution; there are others for which it is not, as will become clear later. In order to make appropriate and hence effective use of CAL and CML, they must be seen in the context of a number of alternative methods of learning. In other words, the computer is one, but only one, of the tools that the teacher can use to help with teaching and learning problems. Educational computing is not particularly special in this respect, and in later chapters analogies will be drawn with the use of other teaching methods and techniques such as individualised programmed instruction, the overhead projector or the use of closed circuit television. A reasonable long-term objective is that teachers should acquire a knowledge of the strengths and weaknesses of the alternative available methods, including computing, so that they may develop appropriate solutions to their problems. An awareness of a technology implies an appreciation of its possibilities and limitations, and how to use it in a given context; it does not imply an in-depth knowledge of its general theory of operation. Hence a detailed understanding of how computers work and how to write computer programs is not a prerequisite for using them effectively in teaching. In some instances it may help by making the teacher more independent of specialist assistance, but the lack of programming skills or an empathy with computers is not, and should not be, a barrier to using them effectively in teaching. Consider, as an analogy, the overhead projector. In order to use an overhead projector successfully, the teacher must learn some basic rules about making and presenting transparencies, but need not know how to design the complex fresnel lens that is at the heart of the device. The aim of the subsequent chapters of this book is to help teachers and trainers develop an awareness of the various aspects of educational computing.

2 COMPUTER ASSISTED LEARNING

Educational Paradigms

In the previous chapter, Computer Assisted Learning (CAL) was described in terms of the kind of information flowing between the student and his learning environment, mediated by the computer. CAL is characterised by a flow of rapidly changing, very detailed, information with the computer playing a prominent role as mediator. However, there are a number of different types of CAL and we must now seek a suitable framework within which to discuss their educational implications. Of the several possible frameworks, that proposed by Kemmis and his colleagues (see Bibliography) is the most useful in this instance. They invented four educational paradigms which they found to be useful in relating computer assisted learning to the general field of education. The four paradigms are:
- the instructional,[†]
- the revelatory,[†]
- the conjectural,[†] and
- the emancipatory.[†]

The Instructional Paradigm

As we have seen, the early forays into computer assisted learning grew out of the use of programmed learning, particularly in North America. Subsequently, the technique was taken up, albeit on a smaller scale, in Europe and the Soviet Union. Behind the practice of programmed learning, lies a theory of conditioning which owes much to Skinner. This proposed that the best way of learning the subject material was to break the learning task into many small tasks and then to concentrate upon each of these in turn. The student would be given a reward to reinforce his learning each time he demonstrated that he had mastered one of these tasks, and would then be allowed to progress to the next. If he encountered problems on a particular task, then he would be held at that point until he had mastered it, or alternatively directed to some remedial work in which the offending task was presented in a different way or possibly broken down into even smaller parts. The key was to divide the subject matter into parts so small that the student had the best possible chance of learning, and his learning was reinforced at every opportunity. Skinner's original theory has since been modified and embodied as part of other more complex theories, but can still be seen as the basis of much of the present-day programmed learning which seeks to rationalise the teaching/learning process, sequencing the presentation of material and emphasising feedback to the student on his performance. The focus of the instruction is on the subject material and on the student's mastery of the various facts and concepts within it.

This approach makes a number of assumptions about the nature of the subject matter; in particular, it assumes that it can be broken up into small parts, each with clearly defined prerequisites and objectives, so that the individual parts can be sensibly structured into a coherent sequence, also with clear prerequisites and objectives. That this is possible is more obvious for some subjects than for others. It also assumes that students conform to the behaviourist learning model. Again, it is not obvious that all of them respond to stimuli in the way that the theory assumes.

Clearly, while the theory of programmed learning may be attractive, its implementation poses a number of problems. The breaking of the subject matter into small, well-defined learning tasks was then, and is still, a highly skilled manual process, placing great demands on the teaching staff. Once the course has been devised, there are still substantial problems of controlling the students' progress through the individual steps, of checking their understanding at each step, and of general management. These latter functions are more easily automated, and it was on them that the early computer assisted learning programs and systems focused.

Instructional Dialogue

The association in teachers' minds of programmed learning with CAL has already been lamented, because, as we have seen, CAL is more than just a means of administering programmed texts. Nevertheless, this form of CAL is probably the most widely known and the most readily appreciated. It is relatively easy to make a computer program which can carry out a very restricted dialogue[†] with a student on a particular subject. A typical, fictitious example is shown in Figure 2.1. In this and similar examples, the computer's side of the dialogue is given in upper case with the student's responses shown in lower case.

This unit of dialogue, sometimes called a frame,[†] relates closely to the typical programmed instruction (PI) unit. It starts with some text for the student to read. In a PI text this would be printed on a page of the book; in the CAL environment it is printed or displayed on the student's computer terminal. At the end of the text the student is asked some questions. It is here that the CAL unit starts to demonstrate its greater flexibility. The PI text can pose questions for the student but must rely on the student's honesty and correct use of the text in checking the answers. In contrast, the CAL program can carry out some limited checking of the student's response and give an appropriate reply.

Figure 2.1: An Example of an Instructional CAL Dialogue

IN AN ATTEMPT TO DEVISE A FRAMEWORK IN WHICH TO DESCRIBE CAL, MCDONALD AND HIS COLLEAGUES 'INVENTED' FOUR PARADIGMS WHICH THEY CALLED
- INSTRUCTIONAL
- REVELATORY
- CONJECTURAL
- EMANCIPATORY
THESE WERE THEN USED IN THEIR EVALUATION OF CAL TO RELATE THE TECHNIQUE TO THE GENERAL FIELD OF EDUCATION

GIVE THE NAMES OF THE FOUR MCDONALD PARADIGMS
? revelatory, conjectural, instructional, emancipatory
VERY GOOD — NOW WHAT DO YOU UNDERSTAND BY THE TERM PARADIGM?
A)   A SELF-CONTRADICTORY STATEMENT
B)   A MODEL OF PERFECTION
C)   AN EXAMPLE OR EXHIBIT
D)   A PLAY ON WORDS
ANSWER A, B, C OR D
? a play on words
PLEASE GIVE YOUR ANSWER AS A, B, C OR D
? d
NO — YOU ARE A LITTLE CONFUSED (OR CYNICAL). A PLAY ON WORDS BY CHANGING ONE OF THE LETTERS IS CALLED A PARAGRAM. THE WORD PARADIGM IS USED HERE TO MEAN AN EXAMPLE

DO YOU WISH TO REVIEW THE DESCRIPTIONS OF THESE PARADIGMS FURTHER?
? no
VERY WELL
.
.
.

The checking is limited to a simple comparison of what the student has typed into his computer terminal and what he was expected to type in. Thus, in the example, the program expected to find the four words 'instructional', 'revelatory', 'conjectural' and 'emancipatory' in some order. When it found them, it printed out a suitable encouraging message and went on to the next question. In this case the student might reasonably answer the question in one of many different ways. It would be impractical to try and foresee all the possible answers and so the student is asked to choose between a number of alternative answers and to respond with a single key letter. When the expected single character was not found, the program did not try to decode the complicated response, but instead reminded the student that he should answer A, B, C or D. The correct response in this case was C, and the CAL package was designed to give an encouraging message if this answer was given. On encountering one of the incorrect alternatives, it provided the student with some feedback on his response, explaining why it was wrong and giving the correct answer.

An alternative form of the multiple choice response[†] is shown at the end of the example where the student is expected to answer 'yes' or 'no'. In this case the package was designed to accept the responses 'y' and 'n' signifying 'yes' and 'no' respectively. At the end of the unit or frame, the computer makes a decision based on the built-in rules specified by the package designer, as to which unit should be presented to the student next. So, although in this simple form of CAL the dialogue between the student and the computer is very restricted, there are obvious improvements in the feedback to the student and in the control of his progress over that which can be achieved with a PI text. It is important to remember that the dialogue, the feedback and the rules which govern the sequence in which the subject material is presented to the student, are under the control of the designer of the CAL package; the use of CAL is not a valid excuse for the teacher to abdicate his educational responsibilities. As a corollary, we must be careful not to confuse those values associated with the learning process with the values of the learning itself. There are two separate areas that must be examined — the educational values behind the organisation and teaching of the subject material, and the means of administering that material to the student. These two areas may be defined as the technology of education and technology in education.

The appeal of this form of CAL is that, once the educational material has been developed and polished, the computer can act as an individual tutor of unlimited patience (albeit of limited intelligence) to each of a large number of students. It is usually seen as a means of reducing the teacher's load in the particular part of the course in which it is used, thus freeing him to devote more effort to those parts which are taught by other means. Hence, while on a small scale it may be viewed as a teacher substitute, when the course is seen as a whole, it is apparent that the CAL component is being used to complement the teacher rather than to replace him.

It was soon clear that the main technological limitation on the instructional form of CAL was the very restricted dialogue available between the student and the computer. The dialogue was restricted both in its ability to match the student's alternative responses against those which had been anticipated by the package writer and also in its field of discourse, in that the computer could only recognise student responses relating to a small part of the subject currently under discussion. Even when the material was structured by the course designer to take advantage of the computer's ability to direct the student along particular paths and so adapt the tutorial to his individual needs, the student was still constrained to follow those prespecified paths embodying the teacher's logic. This constraint was addressed by the later development of the conjectural form of CAL.

The computer's limited ability to match the student's responses appeared to be a less intractable problem and a number of solutions have been produced, ranging from simple keyword matching[†] systems to highly sophisticated systems which can analyse the response to discover its meaning. Unfortunately the sophisticated systems involve a considerable amount of processing by the computer and are often impractical because of the higher costs and the time required to match each response. Consequently most of the CAL systems and packages in common use still have only a limited ability in recognising the student's answers.

Two of the simpler response matching techniques are worthy of brief discussion; examples of their use are shown in Figure 2.2. Again, upper and lower case are used to distinguish between the computer output and the student's responses.

Figure 2.2: Approximate Response Matching

IN THE LIGHT OF THE PREVIOUS DISCUSSION, IS THE USE OF COMPUTER ASSISTED LEARNING INTENDED TO REPLACE THE CLASSROOM TEACHER
? no. it is intended to complement his activities
CORRECT, AS YOU SAY IT IS USED AS A COMPLEMENT TO TEACHER BASED LEARNING

.
.
.

WHERE IS THE EMPHASIS IN THE INSTRUCTIONAL FORM OF CAL
? the emphasis is on the subjcet materal
.
.
.

In the first technique, the computer is directed to identify key words within the student's response that correspond to a prespecified list and then to match the combination of these keywords against the expected patterns. Thus in the first example in Figure 2.2 the words 'no' and 'complement' were identified as significant and indicated that the student answered correctly. Furthermore the student had remembered that CAL is a complement to the teacher. On identifying this correct combination the computer gave the appropriate message. In the second example, the expected keywords 'subject' and 'material' did not appear correctly but were misspelled. Many misspellings can be detected and corrected by the application of a few mechanical rules such as checking for:

- an incorrect character,
- an omitted character,
- an additional, unwanted character,
- a juxtaposition of two adjacent characters.

Other methods in use rely on matching significant constants in the word while ignoring the vowels. When these techniques are used together they can give a powerful means of matching the student's response against a list of expected responses, and while the combination is not as universally accurate as a thorough lexical analysis it does provide an acceptable and practicable solution to the problem.

Drill and Practice

Another use of CAL, Drill and Practice,[†] also falls within the instructional paradigm. In a Drill and Practice lesson the student is presented with a structured succession of exercise questions designed to give him practice in a particular technique. The questions can be written into the CAL package, can be drawn at random from a collection of suitable questions called an item bank[†] or, in some cases, can be generated within the CAL program. This latter approach may be suitable for numerical questions which can consist of skeletons that are completed by the program when the questions are used. The program can provide reasonable random values for the calculation and then determine the correct result for checking the student's response. The sequence of examples can be arranged so as to provide questions of prespecified difficulty, or can be graded in severity to probe the student's learning difficulties. The package can then turn to the simple instructional dialogues discussed earlier to provide remedial tuition in those areas of weakness.

The Revelatory Paradigm

As its name implies, this form of CAL guides the student through a process of learning by discovery in which the subject matter and the underlying theory are progressively revealed to him as he proceeds through the CAL package. Whereas in the instructional form the computer is used to present the subject material, to monitor the student's responses and to control his progress through the course module, in revelatory CAL[†] the computer acts as a mediator between the student and a hidden model[†] of some real-life situation. As the student interacts with the model hidden within the computer he develops a feeling for its behaviour under various circumstances and so is led to discover the rules which govern it. Unlike instructional CAL where the focus is on the subject material and the aim is to optimise the student's mastery of it, this form concentrates much more on the student, and his relationship with the subject as portrayed by the computer.

The use of simulations[†] (and, as we shall see later, model building) is a powerful CAL technique which exploits some of the unique features of the computer as an aid to learning. It enables the student to experiment with situations which would otherwise be too expensive, too time-consuming or impossibly dangerous. It is possible to think of numerous instances, particularly in the natural and social sciences, where it would be educationally useful, yet usually impractical, for the student to have some particular experience. Unlike instructional CAL, where there is usually some other means of administering the subject material, there is often no convenient alternative to the use of a computer based simulation. To give a flavour of the possibilities of this technique we will take a brief look at a few of the wide range of examples currently in educational use.

Simulation in Nuclear Engineering

In the training of nuclear engineers it is desirable for the student to carry out various experiments on the behaviour of nuclear reactors under various conditions. A nuclear reactor is a very expensive piece of laboratory equipment and there is a limit to the number of students who can work on it simultaneously. So these experiments can be very costly. Moreover some of the experiments, for example those which study the criticality of the reactor (when the nuclear reaction becomes self-sustaining and increases in intensity), pose obvious hazards for the safety of the student — and perhaps the surrounding population as well. An experiment which is based upon an accurate computer simulation can demonstrate the desired effects at considerably lower cost — and at less risk to the student or the environment.

Statistics Simulation

In order to give some relevance to the statistics component in a social sciences course the experimental work could be based on a fictitious but consistent set of survey data, devised to correspond to a small imaginary town. This data can then be used to model the behaviour of the people in the town and investigated by the student. Using various statistical techniques he can gain a feel for the validity of each method with different kinds and sizes of sample. Clearly the same sort of experiences could be obtained if the student actually interviewed a large number of people in a suitable town, but considerably more effort would be needed.

Genetics Simulation

Similar considerations apply to the experiments which are commonly carried out in biology courses to demonstrate the laws of genetics. The real experimental work requires that the student should breed selectively a number of generations of an organism and observe the appearance or lack of some characteristic. Even with rapidly maturing insects like fruit flies the experiment lasts for some weeks and requires some considerable experimental skills which may only be incidental to the course. The theory may be taught much more quickly and so the theory and the practical components will be difficult to synchronise. Genetic effects in successive generations can be simulated with the computer very rapidly, so that the student can examine a large number of complex genetic variations and generations in a single lesson. Some experiments in geography or geology run on an even more impractical timescale; processes of mountain formation, volcanic action and erosion typically take aeons, and the only practical way of providing opportunities for this kind of experiment is with a computer model.

Simulated Medical Patients

The final example is drawn from medical education and a course in which the students are required to gain experience in treating patients in various circumstances. This may be achieved by apprenticing the student to an experienced doctor who can lead him through a series of real patients, gradually letting him take more of the decisions, but always on hand to intervene if necessary. Despite its obvious advantages of personal contact and reality this approach has drawbacks. First the variety of real case studies is limited, so that the student may not encounter some rare, but important, situations. Secondly, the number of students that can be apprenticed must be limited if the patient is to be treated and not merely exhibited as a teaching example. Thirdly, the student may make a mistake and, as with experimental work in nuclear physics, mistakes could be fatal. The simulation of patients —

sometimes called 'paper patients' — is not novel; various paper and pencil simulations or games have been devised which allow the student to choose between certain courses of action and then see the consequences of his decisions. The use of the computer to control the simulation reduces the administrative overhead and allows the situation to be made more complex — if this is educationally useful. Further, it allows the simulation to be run against the clock so that, as in the real situation, the student has to consider the time he takes to come to decisions and the delays before his treatments become effective. This improves the impression of reality and hence the student's involvement with the simulation. The use of a 'paper patient' also makes it possible for the student to learn about courses of action that are highly undesirable. This is a unique feature of simulation since the student's experience with real patients must always be constrained to courses of treatment that are beneficial.

Problems of Simulations

It is important to realise that in using computer based simulations for learning the intention is to overcome obstacles such as time, cost or danger, which get between the student and his understanding or feeling for the underlying theory or concepts. In part, this can be achieved by heightening the student's involvement with the simulation — a key factor in this form of CAL — so that he will use his imagination to add in missing details. However, care must be taken to ensure that the orderly model presented in the simulation does not so oversimplify the reality it sets out to explicate that it defeats its own object. When they are used to circumvent experimental difficulties, simulations do not enable the student to acquire experimental skills and so, unless these skills are not required, CAL must remain as a complement to, and not as a replacement for, real experiments — working with a real nuclear reactor, social surveys, insects and mortal patients.

A second problem arises from the assumptions that may be made about the student's encounter with the revelatory CAL package. The package is usually designed to guide the student's investigation of the model along a route which will help him to build the desired concepts of its behaviour. Typically it will assume that the student comes fresh to the simulation before discussing it with his peers who may have already worked through the package. This discussion may well pre-empt the planning and strategy of the package because the student can then outguess the package and so avoid parts of the carefully planned progression through the material.

The Conjectural Paradigm

The use of the educational computer to assist the student in his manipulation and testing of ideas and hypotheses is one of the most exciting forms of CAL, but also perhaps the most difficult to explain and comprehend. It is based on the concept that knowledge can be created through the student's experiences and its emphasis is on the student's exploration of information on a particular topic. This exploration is supported by the computer which is firmly under the student's control. In its simplest form the computer may be used as a calculator[†] to help the student work through complicated arithmetic; at its most complex the CAL package can offer sophisticated tools for modelling real life situations or for manipulating ideas. Because in the conjectural form of CAL[†] it is the student who is in control of the learning rather than the other way about, he is brought much closer to instructing or programming the computer than in the instructional or revelatory forms. This does not necessarily imply that the student and his teachers will tell the computer what to do — program it — with a general purpose programming language. It may be convenient and appropriate to do so, but often it is more satisfactory to provide a simpler means of controlling the computer and one which has been designed specifically for this educational purpose.

One of the criteria which should influence how the student communicates with the computer is the degree of the student's familiarity with the machine and its use. We have stressed the dictum that a knowledge of computing and programming skills should not be prerequisite for successful use of CAL. While this will often lead us away from programming languages that have been designed for programmers, it is not a problem when the students are already studying computing and programming in another part of their course. This is now quite likely if, for example, the student is taking a course in science or technology. Then it may be more convenient and natural for the student to use the programming language with which he is already familiar rather than to learn an alternative one, even though the alternative may be couched in educational terms.

Model Building[†]

The use of the computer as a sophisticated calculating device is such an integral and accepted part of many science and technology courses that it may seem curious to include it under the umbrella of computer assisted learning, or even educational computing. However, it can be argued that since the student is, or should be, learning from his experience, then it is indeed educational. Moreover the step from using the computer as a calculator to modelling real-world systems is relatively small and modelling is certainly a form of CAL. There are many similarities between the processes of simulation used in revelatory CAL and the modelling found in conjectural CAL. Both are concerned with using the computer to emulate some system, process or phenomena so that its behaviour may be investigated and/or predicted. A useful practical distinction is that of the control over the internal working which is given to the student. A student using a CAL simulation may be encouraged to change its external conditions but is prevented from altering (or sometimes even examining) the equations which control its behaviour. On the other hand, in modelling, the student can be asked to specify some parts of the model or to construct the model and then examine its behaviour and see how well it conforms to the real world. Thus the student is able to formulate and test hypotheses about the system he is studying.

As we have already seen, it was to be expected that this form of CAL would find a ready acceptance in many science and technology subjects because the use of the computer is taken for granted and modelling does not appear to be anything out of the ordinary. For example, a student on an electronics or physics course might be asked to write a computer program which modelled the behaviour of a semiconductor junction, to compare his experimental results with those obtained from the model and to comment on any disparities. While this exercise requires a knowledge of semiconductor physics it is not a very demanding programming task and it is reasonable to expect that most students with some programming experience would have few problems in tackling it.

In an environment where the students are not familiar with computers and their programming, it is possible to devise special programs which will facilitate their dialogue with the computer and allow them to build and investigate their own models. This idea has been used with some success in teaching concepts of geometry and shape to young children. The student can instruct the computer to draw lines on the screen of his computer terminal or on a sheet of paper. He controls the length of the lines and after each line can instruct the computer to change direction before drawing the next. Thus by giving the instructions to draw a line of one unit length and then to turn right through ninety degrees a total of four times, the student can obtain the trace of a square. Similar sequences will produce other polygons. By experimentation the student can create a wide variety of patterns and through this experience create his own knowledge of shapes. In the process he will also learn something about problem solving and how to use a computer, but this is really just a useful by-product and is discussed in Chapter 5.

The concept of hypothesis building and testing is not restricted to mathematics, science and technology, but can also be used in less obvious subjects such as history. The study of local history, particularly at secondary level, can involve the manipulation of large amounts of data gleaned from parish registers, commercial directories, census returns and so on. From various pieces of evidence in this store of facts the student is asked to draw some conclusions, to look for additional confirmation and to investigate the limits of his conclusion, that is, to see how far the evidence can be squeezed and where the evidence is too flimsy to support any further inferences. This historical hypothesising can be supported by using the computer to store all the historical data and then to retrieve the relevant facts requested by the student historian. Although the necessary computer programs are quite complex, they can be made quite easy to use and so, once the programs have been made available, there is no need for the teacher or his students to become proficient programmers.

Possibly the most exciting, but as yet the least developed, form of conjectural CAL is based on sophisticated artificial intelligence[†] programs which allow the student to manipulate a wide variety of concepts and to explore logical frameworks. The programs required are derived from research into artificial intelligence and this is partly responsible for the undeveloped state of this form of CAL — it must follow the state of the artificial intelligence art and it is only now that these techniques are becoming viable teaching tools.

The Emancipatory Paradigm[†]

The fourth and last of the CAL paradigms concerns the use of the computer as a means of reducing the workload of the student. McDonald (see Bibliography) distinguishes between two kinds of labour that the student must undertake. There is authentic labour,[†] which is something the student must do as an integral part of his learning and which makes a valuable contribution; there is also inauthentic labour[†] which is necessary as an accessory to the student's learning because it makes his learning possible, but is not an integral part of that learning and is not usually valued for its own sake. So, for example, the student may need to carry out some extensive calculations to obtain the final results from an experiment. While it may be useful for the student to have additional practice at these calculations the important feature of the experiment is the final result – the calculations are not a valued part of the learning experience. Similarly, in the local history example described above, it would be possible for the student to search through all the available data for the relevant evidence, but the mechanics of the search would take considerable time and would not necessarily contribute to his hypothesis, its formation and testing. The computer is a machine which excels at rapid, accurate calculation and information handling, and is a very suitable means of reducing the amount of inauthentic labour in the learning process, supporting the student by providing him with facilities for calculation, information retrieval[†] and so on. As we will see later, it can also be used to support the teacher and trainer in the management of learning.

The teacher must decide the extent to which the labour involved in a particular learning task is authentic or inauthentic. It may play an important role in encouraging the student to think about the problem in a creative way. While it is true that the calculations at the end of a practical experiment or the manual extraction of historical evidence from a mass of data do not contribute directly to the student's learning, they may provide valuable practice in skills which the student will need later. Scientists and engineers need to be able to carry out calculations and historians need to know how to search through census returns and commercial directories, if only so that they will be able to produce the relevant computer programs if need be. We should not become dependent on the omniscient computer. There may also be resistance from the students themselves who have traditionally seen the inauthentic labour as an integral and essential part of the learning task. Thus, carrying out the calculation is in some way a confirmation of the learning they have got from the experiment. If this prop is removed, even though the teacher believes that the underlying principles are thus made more visible, then the students may suspect the value of the learning task.

Serendipity Learning[†]

The use of the computer to support a student's browsing – what might be called computer assisted serendipity – also falls conveniently within this paradigm. The computer could be used to store large quantities of information structured in such a way as to facilitate enquiries on various individual and related topics. It can be programmed to respond on being asked questions by the student, either by regurgitating the relevant pre-stored facts or by indicating the whereabouts of the appropriate sources of information. The structuring of the information within the computer can allow the student to explore a particular subject in depth or move to associated topics. The mass of raw information and the cross-linking necessary to support the browsing activity is vast and, unless the topics are severely restricted, needs phenomenal resources to set up before the system is fully usable.

The problem is being addressed by research work in artificial intelligence which seeks to model the way in which we, as sentient human information processors, behave. Over our lifetimes and particularly during the early years of childhood and formal education, we receive, collate and store large quantities of information without consciously adding it to our knowledge and setting it into a particular structure. The search then is for a machine that will learn in a reasonable approximation to a human being, but without a human's imperfections. The stored information could then be accessed by students and form the basis for an ideal serendipity system. Each time a student held a dialogue with the system the knowledge of the system would be increased. It would be possible to replicate the stored knowledge of the system by electronic means and so produce teaching machines that could learn. Alas, there are a number of problems with this vision of the ideal serendipity system. Firstly, with the existing level of technology, our computers are neither sufficiently powerful to run such complex programs quickly nor sufficiently large to store all the data required. Secondly, we have speculated that we can produce a system that behaves like a human being in structuring and storing information, with all the advantages and yet none of the human fallibilities such as partial or inaccurate recall. These aims may be mutually incompatible: in other words a learning machine may need some way of forgetting and may not forget in the way that we would like it to forget. Thirdly, given that our fundamental aim is to assist with the student's learning, we should ask whether this is the best way to achieve that aim and an appropriate use of the technology. At present, and for the medium-term future, computer assisted serendipity is useful and effective in a restricted context, for example, to help the student survey key literature on a specific subject, but its general use in an environment where no restrictions would be placed on the range of subjects or the level of detail must await developments in artificial intelligence research.

In practice the emancipatory form of CAL usually appears as an adjunct to another use and it may be difficult to decide which of the forms predominates. Many of the CAL applications described above, for example the simulations in social science and biology, the use of 'paper patients' in medical education, the retrieval of information[†] from a mass of historical data and the calculations involved in modelling a real world system, could be carried out without the use of a computer, relying on manual, inauthentic labour for their computations. Some of course, would be quite impractical, given the timescale of the learning process. Often the teacher is attracted by a characteristic of just one of the four types of CAL. This can then provide the trigger for the change in curriculum or teaching methods. Then other advantages can be exploited and the new learning package may contain features of different kinds of CAL, appropriately combined and further complemented by other non-CAL teaching media.

The Rationale for CAL

Each of the four types of CAL exploits various features of the computer to assist in the teaching and learning process and, in particular, uses the computer to provide learning opportunities which would be difficult or impractical to provide in any other way. Thus, in the instructional form, the computer is used as a patient tutor; in the revelatory form it is used to mediate between the student and a hidden model or simulation of a real world situation; in the conjectural form it helps the student to formulate and test his hypotheses; in the emancipatory form it reduces the amount of non-essential work he must do to reach his learning objectives. In all its forms it can provide a more active partner for the student in his pursuit of learning than would be possible with other teaching media such as books, programmed instruction texts, tape slide and the like. At the same time the student can feel that he is only exposing his learning problems and weaknesses to a machine which in some way does not matter, rather than to his tutor or his peers who do. So in addition to the possibilities of individualising instruction, the student can feel protected from his mistakes rather than exposed by them and encouraged to experiment with fewer inhibitions.

CAL may be perceived as optimising the student's performance towards prespecified goals — the use of a technology of education to centre the course on the subject material, or seen as a way of optimising the instruction towards the student's own goals — the use of technology in education to centre the course firmly on the student. We should be clear as to the aim of our use of the technology in any given situation. To return to a recurrent theme of this text, we must be careful to distinguish between the value of the technology and the value of the learning that we seek to facilitate by its use. If CAL is to be used effectively, then it must be used appropriately, that is where it offers learning opportunities which could not easily be provided in any other way.

3 USING COMPUTER ASSISTED LEARNING

In the previous chapter we discussed the various ways in which CAL could assist in the learning process and concluded that, if it was to be used appropriately and hence effectively, it should be used to provide teaching and learning which could not easily be made available by other means. This chapter is concerned with the production of CAL packages and their integration into the curriculum and the teaching/learning process.

The Cal Package

CAL, like other educational technologies and teaching methods, has various unique qualities and should be seen in the context of alternative methods of learning, each of which has its own useful qualities. It is one, but only one, of the tools that the teacher can use to help with his teaching and learning problems. It follows therefore that CAL will be one but only one, of the components of a complete learning package. Typically it will support, or be supported by, printed materials, lectures or tutorials; sometimes it may be used in conjunction with other non-book media. There are three reasons for using a variety of media:
 — appropriate use,
 — financial constraints,
 — variety.
As we have seen, each medium should be used appropriately to obtain the greatest benefit from it. For example, the background information required by the student prior to carrying out a CAL simulation could be presented as part of the CAL program on the student's terminal or could be printed as a set of student notes which the student could study away from the terminal. It may be more appropriate to adopt the latter approach rather than to use the computer as an automated page turner. Secondly, the appropriate use of technology is bound by financial constraints. While printed material is relatively cheap, the use of CAL and other aids such as closed-circuit television is admittedly expensive and therefore must be deployed with care so as to be cost-effective. At the same time, teachers are also very expensive and they too must be employed appropriately. Finally, the variety obtained by using a combination of different media and teaching styles can help to retain the student's enthusiasm and interest in his learning. A course which consists only of a series of CAL programs where the student inter-

acts only with a computer terminal, could be as boring as a course based only on lectures where the student sits with several score of his peers listening to a speaker at the opposite end of a lecture theatre and often remote in both distance and empathy.

Print Media

Books and student notes are cheap to produce or buy and are durable. They do not require any special equipment for their use (except by the blind or partially sighted) and, being small and portable, can be used almost everywhere. Because they are cheap they can be retained by the student. They are reliable in that they do not go wrong and even if damaged, for example by having coffee spilled on them, they are still usable. However, they are passive aids to learning; the student may respond to the book but the book cannot detect whether the student is having difficulty with a particular topic and modify its approach to try a different strategy. With careful design, a programmed instruction text may go some way towards alleviating this problem, but the printed word remains essentially passive and static.

Tape Slide

The combination of tape and slide is also a passive medium but one which gives a large information bandwidth; in other words the student can receive information at a fast rate by looking at pictures and listening. The use of sound recording also allows the author to inject more variety and realism into the presentation. The sound track can thus include recordings of different people and situations instead of printed quotations and word pictures. The costs are higher than for printed materials so that each copy must be re-used rather than retained by the student for future reference. The technique requires some equipment, which can be made relatively simple and reliable. Although it is portable, it is inconvenient to use it away from the student's study base. It is more sensitive to damage than printed materials.

Video

Video recorded and film material offer further improvements in the speed and quality of presentation of material. The animation affords greater impact on the audience and the means of explaining moving phenomena. But the costs of production and delivery are much greater than for printed materials or tape slide, the equipment is more complex and less reliable and is also not portable, so that it is confined to a given study area. Although the student can view a particular sequence an unlimited number of times, the medium is still passive because it cannot respond differently to each student or vary its approach to take account of a student's individual problems.

Lecturers, Tutors and Instructors

Teachers and instructors are very versatile teaching devices. Their outstanding ability is their adaptability which even for a poor teacher potentially exceeds that of the best adaptive CAL package. A teacher is able to sense and probe a student's learning difficulties and then to try a succession of different strategies, either singly or in combination, in an attempt to overcome the problem. Moreover, the teacher can learn from his previous encounters with students and the course material and so evolve new methods of presentation. The teacher is versatile and, while his specialism may be limited to one or two broad subject areas, he can teach a large number of topics within those areas. He can usually also teach a much wider range of subjects at lower levels. The teacher is largely self-programming, in that he can prepare his own lessons with the minimum of external support from an educational development unit or audiovisual production team. Teachers can operate with unsophisticated equipment, such as a blackboard and chalk or an overhead projector, but will often use these only as ancillaries and most can, if necessary, teach without any extra equipment at all. They are easy to produce but difficult to train and once in use are expensive to keep. Intelligence, adaptability and versatility have their price. Since the training of a teacher takes several years, there is a considerable delay between the realisation that demand is increasing and the response of an increased supply. Teachers are reliable but prone to minor failures or illnesses which may render them inoperative or less efficient for a few days.

However, while teachers are the most effective all round teaching devices they do have some drawbacks to offset their many virtues. Because of their high cost their availability is limited, so that it is not usually possible to have just a few students for each teacher. The teacher's ability to adjust his teaching to the needs of individual students, and hence his effectiveness, can be seriously diluted in large group lecturing. The problem is compounded by the administrative load which inevitably falls on our teachers and reduces the time that they can spend with their students. This may be alleviated by using the computer to assist with the management of learning as discussed in Chapter 4. The second drawback is the teacher's limited presentation bandwidth. Although the teacher is very adaptable, by himself he can only impart information to his students by speech and gestures. This makes it difficult for him to explain visual phenomena or the functioning of dynamic systems, unless he makes use of other media to support these parts of the course. Thirdly, because his speed of calculation is limited, the teacher's explication of real world systems may have to be calculated in advance and hence be less flexible.

Computers

Computers are less flexible devices for supporting learning than teachers but they are nevertheless a great improvement on other media. Their key feature is their ability to process information, to carry out calculations and to mediate in the flow of information between the student and his learning environment quickly and accurately. This ability can be used to provide the student with an infinitely patient tutor, to simulate and model real world systems with textual or animated diagrammatic output, or to reduce the amount of inessential labour involved in the student's learning. But CAL is not a universal panacea for all learning problems. It requires expensive equipment which is only semiportable. The equipment is complex and so not completely reliable. The CAL materials are not easily damaged (damage in this context is rather different from the sort of damage that might be done to a book or video-tape) but even slight damage will make the program unusable. CAL's main drawback is its cost, which falls somewhere between the low cost of printed material and the high cost of individual or small group tuition. The costs of CAL and the ways in which they may be reduced are discussed in more detail in Chapter 6.

The Multimedia Package

Thus we come to the concept of a learning package† which consists of a number of different contributions to a specific topic, using a variety of media in an appropriate combination. It is often argued that the use of CAL replaces the teacher with technology and thus dehumanises the learning process. This is certainly true of any attempt to replace the teacher, whether it be by CAL, educational television or the exclusive use of programmed learning, and it is unquestionably undesirable. Education is essentially a social process involving interaction between human beings. However, the central thesis of this text is that CAL should be used appropriately to complement rather than to replace the teacher. The multimedia package will therefore usually include a contribution from the teacher as well as from the computer. In those cases where CAL is the dominant component, the whole may be regarded as a CAL package.† This package is distinct from the CAL program† which is that part of the package administered by the computer. The program is sometimes referred to by CAL practitioners as 'courseware',[†] forming a triad with its computing partners 'hardware'[†] and 'software'.[†]

Producing CAL Packages

There is much similarity between the production of CAL packages and of packages involving other media. The production process illustrated in Figure 3.1 starts with a specification of the educational or training objectives of the whole package and is followed by the overall design of the package.

It is at this stage that the designer must be aware of the strengths and weaknesses of the various techniques and resources at his disposal so that he can make informed decisions about the complementary roles of each of the different contributions. He must specify the objectives and the strategy of each contribution and thus determine, in the case of the CAL program, the blend of different forms of CAL (instructional, revelatory, conjectural, emancipatory) that will be used. From this overall design can come the detailed design of the individual contributions, including the CAL program.

In the previous chapter we discussed various kinds of CAL from an education viewpoint. Now we should consider the different ways in which the student can interact with the computer and use the CAL program. These have major implications for the educational strategy which is to be used, but are also constrained by practical considerations of what is technically feasible and available in the right place at the right time.

Presenting CAL Packages

The traditional picture of CAL in most people's minds is that of a student seated in front of a computer terminal,[†] reading messages displayed on the screen of the terminal or typed out on a roll of paper, and typing his responses on a keyboard rather like that of an ordinary typewriter. This kind of display is illustrated in Figure 2.1. This is also the most common way of giving students access to the computer but is not necessarily the most effective in all circumstances. The basic terminal, which can display only a limited range of characters including letters, digits and a number of common symbols, can be replaced by a more sophisticated (though more expensive) device which can also draw pictures, diagrams, graphs and so on, as a series of lines. This greatly widens the possibilities for presenting complex information as shown in Figure 3.2, and improves the attractiveness and the quality of the teach-

Figure 3.1: The Production of CAL Packages

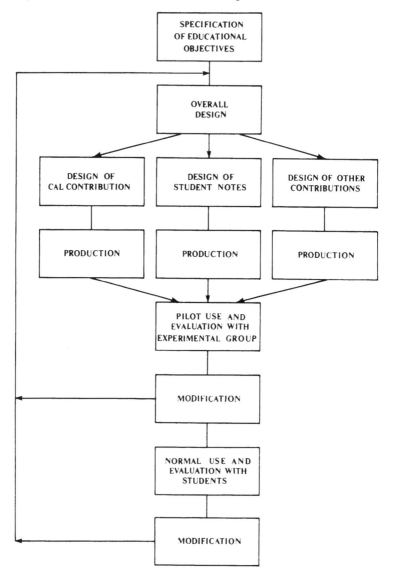

Figure 3.2: An Example of CAL Using Graphics

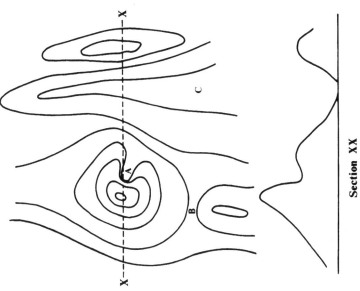

STUDY THE CONTOUR MAP SHOWN ON THE RIGHT.

WHAT IS THE NAME OF THE FEATURE AT POINT A
? a cwm
YES, THAT IS THE WELSH NAME. AN ALTERNATIVE
NAME IS A CIRQUE

Section XX

ing – although not necessarily the quality of the learning – albeit at a greater cost.

It is possible to devise simple diagrams made out of character patterns using character (or alphameric) terminals,[†] but the results are usually less satisfactory. Some picture (or graphics) terminals[†] can display animated diagrams which may further enhance the package. Similar effects can be obtained with film or videotape, but both of these media are passive whereas CAL can respond to the student's behaviour. For example, a simulation of some dynamic system could be illustrated in a video package but only with predetermined system parameters. With a CAL simulation the student can specify and control the parameters and observe the changing results displayed in a diagrammatic form on his graphics terminal.

Both alphameric and graphics terminals are standard pieces of computing equipment – although this does not imply that they are widely available in educational and training institutions. There have been a number of projects in various countries to develop a special purpose terminal for CAL which could handle a number of different media, all under computer control, at one student learning station. Since the computer can instruct the terminal to print a certain character or to draw a line in a certain position, there is no technical reason why it should not also be able to instruct the terminal to select and display a certain photographic slide or microfiche image, to play a certain sound recording on a tape recorder or to synthesise a short verbal message to the student. In general these multi-media terminals have not been widely used because of their greater cost and because of the educational complexity in designing effective teaching packages that will use the facilities.

A number of alternative ways of allowing the student to give his response to the computer terminal have also been investigated. These range from the provision of some extra keys on the keyboard for indicating frequently used responses such as 'yes', 'no', 'don't know', 'help', 'go on to the next part' or 'go back to the last part', to a special screen which displays the computer output and can also sense when and where the student touches it. This allows the student to indicate various words in the displayed text or a specific part of a diagram. These simpler alternative methods of input to the terminal have proved useful, particularly with students who are not proficient typists and so find keyboard input an unnecessary hindrance to using CAL.

Perhaps we should ask whether it is reasonable that the development of keyboard skills should be a part of our students' basic training, as other study techniques are. It is at least arguable that typing is an artificial impediment, imposed only by some computer based methods of teaching and training.

Interactive† or Batch Computing†

Interactive terminals provide an immediacy of access and a rapid, almost instant, feedback for the CAL user. But they are not the only way nor are they the cheapest way of communicating with a computer. An alternative approach is for the student to prepare his input away from the computer and to write it down on a form. The data is then prepared so that it can be read by the computer and takes its turn in a queue of jobs waiting to be run. After it has been processed by the computer the output is returned to the student. The delay between the student preparing his input and receiving his output can vary from several minutes to several days, depending on the computer used and the time taken to move the information from the student to the computer and back again. In some situations the delay may be educationally acceptable so that the additional costs of providing terminals for the students are not justified. For example, in a business game where several teams are in competition to manage their simulated companies most profitably, it may be convenient to collect all the teams' decisions for the current step together and then process them on the computer. While the teams await their results they can start on the lengthy process of planning their decisions for the next step. If the economic constraints are such that terminals are not available the CAL designer will be forced to use this less immediate form of access and design his educational tactics accordingly.

As indicated previously, the traditional picture of CAL has a single student sitting at each terminal so that the computer acts as a mediator between the student and his learning environment. This was the model proposed in Chapter 1 and illustrated again in Figure 3.3a.

While it may be the most suitable arrangement for instructional CAL it provides a very solitary, if individualised, environment for the student. In many circumstances, in revelatory and conjectural CAL, it is advantageous for students to work in pairs as shown in Figure 3.3b. Educationally this can enrich the CAL lesson, because the students can now discuss their progress with each other and so help each other with their problems, understanding and hypotheses. The students can learn as much, if not more, from their dialogue together, as from the supportive CAL package which may recede into a more passive role, prompting the students and verifying their hypotheses. As we shall see later, a major factor in the cost of CAL is the provision of computer terminals. An arrangement where two students work on a CAL package at a single terminal

Figure 3.3a: Single Student CAL

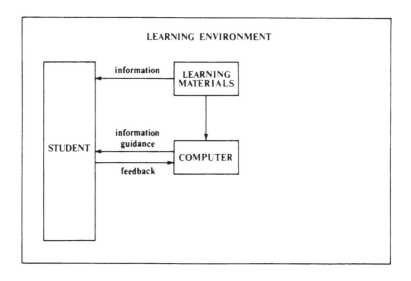

Figure 3.3b: Student Pair CAL

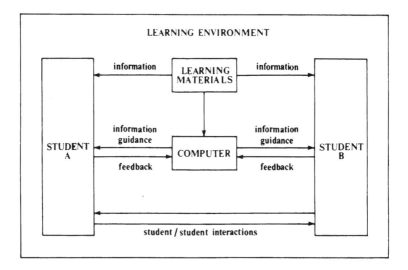

can give substantial savings in the computing resources required.

Structuring the Material

There are direct parallels between the detailed design of a CAL package and the design of packages using other media. The designer must start with a clear understanding of what, educationally, the package is required to do, and then keep these educational objectives clearly in view while exploiting the strengths and circumventing the weaknesses of each medium. Whereas the designer of a programmed instruction text is working with printed words and diagrams, and the designer of a tape slide sequence operates with a commentary and a set of pictures, the CAL author is producing a structured series of short dialogues between the student or students and the computer, perhaps augmented with diagrams that will be displayed on the terminal and other materials such as printed student notes. The dialogue is not spoken, but printed on the terminal and typed by the student; this has implications for the phraseology in the same way that a written commentary can sound stilted when it is spoken on a tape.

A significant difference between CAL and many other media is the ability of a CAL package to break out of a linear sequence of material to recap or offer an alternative approach, to allow the student to change something in his model or simulation and so to respond to his individual preferences. This requires that the package material be very carefully structured so that the student can follow sensible paths through the lesson. There are probably an infinite number of different ways in which students could study a particular topic but it is not possible to devise a package so that it will satisfy most of the students for most of the time, while remaining of manageable size and complexity.

A useful design technique here is to set out the various objectives in diagrammatic form as a directed graph, indicating the ordering and relationships between them as shown in Figure 3.4a. This can then be structured into a basically linear progression through the course material such as tutorial sessions or experiments with a computer model. Each of the sections can be broken down further into smaller modules and elaborated with alternative or additional branches if necessary, as shown in Figures 3.4b and 3.4c.

The CAL Production Team

The sheer quantity of dialogue and structure in many CAL packages poses production problems which different authors and institutions have sought to overcome in different ways:

Figure 3.4a: Part of a Directed Graph Showing the
Ordering of Learning Objectives

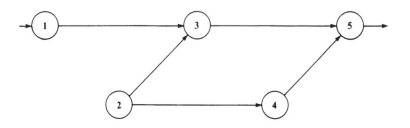

Figure 3.4b: A Linear Progression Through the
Same Ordered Objectives

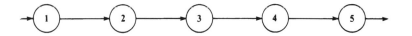

Figure 3.4c: Further Elaboration of the Course, with Branching

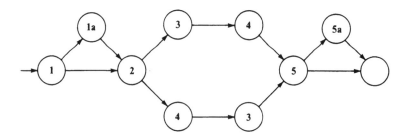

    — by providing specialist CAL authors,
    — by encouraging teachers to produce their own materials,
    — by setting up hybrid production teams.

One school of thought says that the actual production of the material should be undertaken by a CAL specialist who can take a detailed educational design from the teacher and turn it into a draft package. Another advocates that facilities should be made available for teachers to produce their own materials. The first group argue that it is wasteful for teachers to develop the production and programming skills necessary to write and check the sequences of instructions to the computer; it is much more efficient for this process to be handled by a specialist author[†] who is very familiar with the techniques required and any problems that may be encountered. This argument is countered by the second group who point out that the cost of employing a specialist is a luxury many institutions cannot afford and who maintain that it is possible for teachers to carry out the work themselves, if they are provided with the necessary tools. They claim that it is preferable for the teacher to have the detailed knowledge and control over the package which is possible if he himself produces it. As with the production of other media, both sides can be right in different circumstances; the choice depends on the complexity of the package, the level of specialist support available and the proficiency of the teacher. One hybrid production method, which has been used with some success in North America, involves teachers, secretaries, CAL specialists, and sometimes also the students. The teacher dictates the basic dialogue and structure of the package to a secretary who then constructs the bulk of the package from his notes. Where there are complexities beyond his abilities, the secretary inserts a note to this effect with details of what is required. The embryonic package is then taken over by the CAL specialist who attends to any parts which the secretary could not write and generally smoothes off the rough edges before handing it back to the teacher for inspection and evaluation.

A package which relies solely on printed materials or tape slide materials is largely self-explanatory in that little or none of its construction is hidden from the teacher. In a CAL package, however, there are a number of things relating to the computer program which must be written down for the benefit of those who may wish to change it at some later date. The production of this documentation[†] is a very necessary, and not too arduous, task which will be more than justified if the CAL package is to be used by another institution or if some later changes must be made.

The central figure in the CAL production team is the teacher, who may be supported by a number of other people. The role of the CAL specialist is to advise on, and assist with, various aspects of production as described above. Some teams include an educational psychologist or, more generally, a specialist in educational development, who can advise on educational strategy in the course as a whole and on the package in particular. Here again there are more similarities in, than differences between, the production of CAL packages and that of packages based on other media. One unusual contributor found in a very few teams is a student. His function is to advise on the strategy and presentation of the material from a recipient's point of view. This is clearly a neglected but vital role which could well be included in many more production teams, not only in the area of CAL.

Evaluation

The evaluation of a learning package often poses problems for the teacher who needs to know, in detail, how the students work through the material, so that he can uncover any problem areas or deficiencies. The task of evaluating a CAL package, or at least the CAL component of the package, can be considerably eased because the computer itself can keep comprehensive records of the students' work. Indeed the ease with which this data can be collected can make a fresh problem, that of determining what is useful from the mass of what is available, such as:

    — the student's route through the package,
    — the student's responses at various points,
    — the time taken by the student in studying each part of the package.

The package can also encourage the student to provide feedback on parts that he found difficult or unclear, and then to collect and collate these comments for the evaluators. Generally it is more satisfactory to allow the student the opportunity of registering his comments or grievances as he works through the lesson, rather than to wait until he has completed it and then elicit the information at an interview. The range of information collected automatically can then be used to complement data obtained by observation and interviews, and performance data from pre- and post-testing. The overall CAL package is first evaluated with a small, pilot group of students and in the light of the evaluation may be modified as shown in Figure 3.1. Because some of the evaluation mechanisms can be built into the program it is possible for the evaluation to be a continual process throughout the time the material is used by students. This provides further possibilities for improving the quality of the learning.

As we have seen, the appropriate and most effective applications of CAL are in areas which exploit the unique qualities of the medium. CAL can often provide learning opportunities which are very different from those which would be found in a course taught by other means; sometimes there are parts of the course which would be impractical without the use of a CAL simulation or some other form of computer support. Hence it can be misleading to carry out a quantitative comparison between the learning resulting from a CAL package and from, say, a lecture based lesson. Any comparison should examine the qualitative aspects of using CAL as a component in the package, to determine whether CAL is the best educational tool to use in the given circumstances.

4 COMPUTER MANAGED LEARNING

Rationale

The basic rationale of Computer Managed Learning (CML) is an attempt to relieve the teacher or trainer of various tedious and time-consuming management tasks and so leave him with more time to devote to the essence of teaching. In an ideal CML environment, there would be a smooth partnership between the teacher, the student and the computer, in which each performed those tasks most suited to their (its) abilities. The teacher, freed of the administrative burden, would be able to devote his time to the task of helping students for which he was trained, and hopefully enjoys; the student would enjoy a course of study which was tailored to his individual needs and preferences, with ample feedback to guide his studies; the computer, having no need of job satisfaction, but able to process information quickly and accurately, would take over the routine management of the courses.

The computer is therefore here cast in a background, supportive role in which it helps to manage, rather than to provide, learning opportunities. As we shall see later, the functions which it carries out are not complex, but require the accurate handling and processing of large amounts of information. They could be carried out equally well by a small team of clerical assistants appointed to support each teacher — if the resources were available to recruit and pay these extra staff. It is argued that a CML system is more cost-effective than clerical staff, or than using qualified teaching staff for routine management. The argument is strengthened by an application of the Peter Principle which, if applied to this case, holds that each teacher or trainer will be promoted to the level of his incompetence. Thus the more able teachers are promoted to positions of responsibility in which they will spend more time managing and hence less time doing the teaching which they are good at. While good teachers may also be able administrators, it is curious that their promotion tends to deny the organisation the skills for which they were promoted. Clearly, while CML is not a universal panacea, it is worth examining its possibilities and limitations as a solution to this problem, and as a means of improving the effectiveness of the management of teaching and learning.

The CML Cycle

There are four broad areas in which the computer may be used to provide management support. Firstly, it can construct, mark and analyse tests for diagnostic or assessment purposes. Second, it can keep records of the students' performance and progress through their courses. Third, based on what is known about each student and the structure of the course, it can provide individual guidance for each student, directing or advising him on his choice of route through structured course materials. Finally, from its records, it can report on the performance and progress of the students and of the course to the individual students, the tutors and the managers of the education or training institution. Individual CML systems vary in their coverage of this range of functions; some provide comprehensive facilities for general management, while others are concerned with one aspect only, for example, test marking, analysis and construction. As we shall see, the general purpose systems may still be restricted in their ability to handle a wide variety of course structures and so may be limited to a particular subject area or type of student.

The majority of CML systems embody a model of student study behaviour which, in a simplified form is shown in Figure 4.1. The student enters a cycle in which he first studies a learning module and is then assessed on his understanding of the module. The computer processes the test and, based on the results and what is already known about the student and the course structure, advises the student and his tutor on the choice of a next module. The cycle is completed as the student begins to study the new module. At the start of the course, the student is directed to the first module and then injected into the cycle; he leaves it when he has finished the course. A more general model which relates the concurrent activities of the student, his tutor, and the computer is shown in Figure 4.2. Even this leaves much to be desired, both administratively and educationally. It does however, provide a framework on which to hang the following, more detailed discussion of the various aspects of computer managed learning.

Assessment

The process of assessment is at the heart of most CML systems and is the function which initially attracts most new users of the technology. Its appeal is easy to explain. The traditional process of assessment involves the teacher in a lengthy task of marking tests by hand. The student gains little from taking the test because the effort required to provide him with any more feedback than just a final score is too great. Perhaps the best that can usually be achieved is a group tutorial in which common problems are discussed. Certainly with very favourable staff-student ratios, the tutor can take his students through the test, point by point,

Figure 4.1: The Simplified Computer Managed Learning Cycle

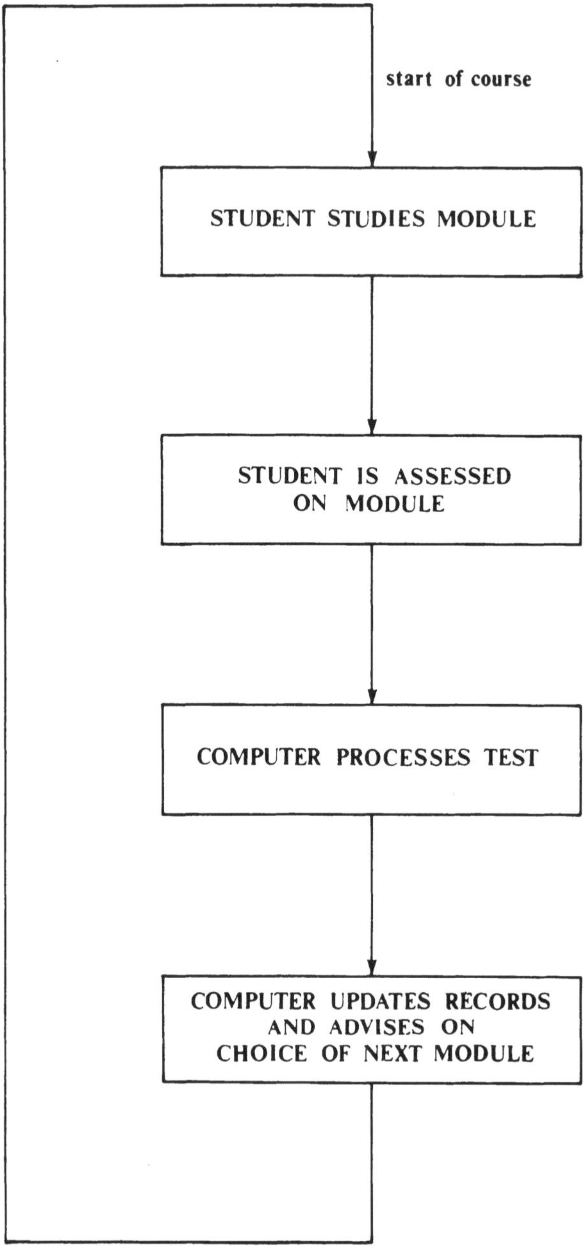

start of course

```
┌──────────────────────────────────┐
│      STUDENT STUDIES MODULE      │
└──────────────────────────────────┘

┌──────────────────────────────────┐
│      STUDENT IS ASSESSED         │
│          ON MODULE               │
└──────────────────────────────────┘

┌──────────────────────────────────┐
│     COMPUTER PROCESSES TEST      │
└──────────────────────────────────┘

┌──────────────────────────────────┐
│   COMPUTER UPDATES RECORDS       │
│        AND ADVISES ON            │
│    CHOICE OF NEXT MODULE         │
└──────────────────────────────────┘
```

Figure 4.2: A More General Model of Computer Managed Learning

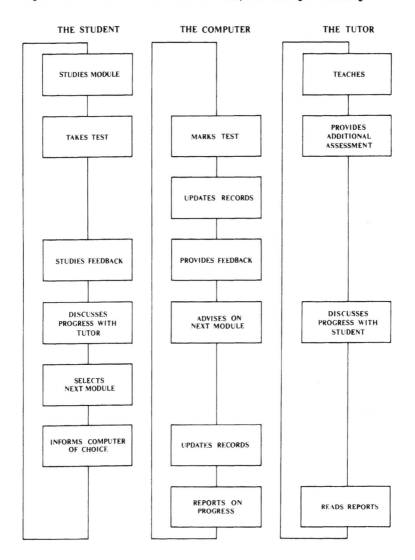

but this is now the exception rather than the rule. The tutor also gains little from the assessment. While a good teacher may form a subjective opinion of how the students are progressing, it is often difficult to see the wood from the trees. Some teachers do enjoy marking tests by hand, but for the majority it is a tedious chore that must be endured. Further, there is the possibility, or for some the probability, of making errors in the adding up and recording of marks.

Multiple Choice Tests

The introduction of new forms of assessment, particularly the use of multiple choice question (MCQ) tests,[†] stimulated the development of techniques for marking tests with the aid of a computer. In the simple form of a MCQ, the student is posed a question and is asked to select one from a list of alternative answers which follows the question. One of these is the 'correct' answer and the rest are used as distractors, devised to appear credible to students who cannot determine the answer accurately. The MCQ can appear in a variety of forms such as:

 — choose one response from several alternatives,
 — choose two or more responses from the alternatives,
 — determine whether a statement is true or false,
 — match two lists of items.

Some examples are shown in Figure 4.3.

Apart from being amenable to automatic marking techniques, MCQ tests have two main advantages over short answer[†] or essay-type questions. Firstly, because the student need only indicate the answer of his choice instead of constructing a response, more questions can be answered in a given time. Thus a larger part of the syllabus can be tested. Secondly, since the person marking the test is given no latitude in the way in which he marks, the test is marked in the same way for all and can be more objective than a test with constructed responses. MCQ tests are therefore attractive when large student populations must be tested to a uniform standard. They also suffer from several drawbacks. By their nature, they do not test the students' ability to form their thoughts into a written response, and it is difficult to devise questions which will test the students' powers of deduction and reasoning. The testing of their factual recall is rather easier. Perhaps the greatest problem with MCQ tests is to devise good questions which test the right things, are unambiguous, and will provide evidence about the students' learning problems from the way in which they are answered. Even if an essay question is badly set, many of the students will be able to attempt an answer and it is possible to rectify the situation with sympathetic marking. In an

Figure 4.3: Examples of Multiple Choice Questions

Question 1.   In which year did Schubert write his Mass in E flat?

a. 1830
b. 1825
c. 1828
d. 1822

Question 2.   Which of the following integers are prime numbers?

a. 39
b. 7
c. 13
d. 2

Question 3.   Larbonism is a method used in the teaching of remedial reading. Is this statement true or false?

a. true
b. false

Question 4.   Match the following countries with their capital cities.

a. France   1. Dublin
b. England   2. Paris
c. Scotland   3. Edinburgh
d. Wales   4. London
e. Eire   5. Cardiff

MCQ test, there is no latitude for error. If a question is ambiguously framed, then the damage is done when the students answer it — there is little possibility for recovery later. Writing good multiple choice questions or items requires skill and considerable practice. Even with experienced question-writers it is reasonable to expect that two out of three questions will prove unsatisfactory in their original form. Fortunately the format of the questions is amenable to analysis which makes it possible to distinguish between good and bad questions. Unsatisfactory questions can then be examined and either modified or rejected. A by-product of most CML test-marking systems is an analysis of the performance of the test and each item in it.

Computer Aided Marking

The marking of short answer and essay-type questions[†] requires the examiner to read the response and identify various key words and ideas contained in it. The deciphering of the handwriting, recognition of words and phrases and matching the constructed response against the model answer, is a complex process requiring considerable intelligence on the part of the examiner. In general, the automatic reading and assessment of such answers is impractical. However, the format of MCQ tests is much simpler for machine reading and checking. Where a large number of MCQ test papers are to be marked by hand, the students' answer sheets can be printed with a number of groups of boxes, one group for each question in the test. Each possible response to the question is associated with a particular box, and the student is asked to answer each question by making a mark, perhaps a cross, in the appropriate box, as shown in Figure 4.4.

Figure 4.4: Examples of Multiple Choice Questions for Automated Marking

Instructions: place a cross in the appropriate box to indicate the answer or answers you think correct.

Question 1.   In which year did **Schubert** write his Mass in E flat?

            a. 1830   a ☐
            b. 1825   b ☐
            c. 1828   c ☐
            d. 1822   d ☐

Question 2.   Which of the following integers are prime numbers?

            a. 39   a ☐
            b.   7   b ☐
            c. 13   c ☐
            d.   2   d ☐

Question 3.   Larbonism is a method used in the teaching of remedial reading. Is this statement true or false?

                                             true ☐
                                            false ☐

Question 4.   Match the following countries with their capital cities.

                                                    a b c d e
            a. France   1. Dublin   1 ☐
            b. England   2. Paris   2 ☐
            c. Scotland   3. Edinburgh   3 ☐
            d. Wales   4. London   4 ☐
            e. Eire   5. Cardiff   5 ☐

To facilitate marking the test, the examiner can then prepare a template in the same format as the students' answer sheets, with a hole in each of the correct answer boxes. When the template is laid over a completed answer sheet, those answers which are in the correct boxes will be visible through the holes in the template. This is analogous to the way in which MCQ tests can be read and marked by a computer. Instead of holes in a template, the specially designed and printed answer sheets are 'read' by a machine connected to the computer. This machine, called an optical mark reader,[†] determines the pattern of responses made by the student. The computer then matches this pattern against the prespecified correct pattern and scores the test. The computer's ability to perform this operation extremely quickly and accurately, makes it possible to devise more sophisticated marking schemes. Thus the examiner can use variable scoring, penalty scoring or confidence levels, if he feels that this would make the test more meaningful, useful or reliable. For some questions there may be no one clearly 'correct' answer, but rather a number of answers which are more or less correct. In this case, the 'better' answers can be made to yield higher scores than the 'worse' ones. Penalty scoring is an extreme case in which some responses are so wrong that the examiner wishes to penalise the student by deducting marks. It may also be used to deter the candidates from guessing at the correct answer; marks will not be lost if the question is not attempted, but will be deducted if an incorrect answer is given. In practice it appears that although penalty scoring does reduce guessing, it has very little effect on the overall quality of the test. The examiner may wish to determine how confident the student is in his answer, by including a supplementary question which allows the student to indicate whether he is very certain, reasonably certain, or doubtful about his response. His score on the question is then multiplied by some factor which depends on his level of confidence. If he is correct and very certain then he will score more than if he is correct but doubtful. The multiplication factor is also applied to the penalty scores for incorrect answers so that a question answered incorrectly and confidently will be penalised more than a dubious, incorrect response. The student's set of responses can also be matched against the test rubrick to provide an accurate check on whether the right combination of questions has been answered.

The spread of MCQ tests and the development of CML test marking proceeded together. The more cynical might ask whether the growth of MCQ was primarily because of its educational value – or because it facilitated the use of the computer. Certainly, given the wide range of facilities which are possible when a computer is used for marking, the MCQ test is a very powerful tool for assessment, but it is a tool which complements rather than replaces short answer and essay-type tests. Although constructed responses are not, with one exception, easy to score by machine, they have not thus been made obsolete by the MCQ test. The criterion should be that the technique is educationally appropriate, not whether it fits easily in an automated testing system. The exception referred to is the marking of arithmetic tests where it is feasible to ask the student to give his answers in a form which can be read by a machine. In other subjects the easiest way of handling short answer and essay questions is to mark them by hand and then put the resulting scores or grades into the CML system.

Feedback

The student's assessment may be used by the organisation to determine how well he is progressing in relation to the course, his peers or some set standard. It may be used for the benefit of the student himself, to give him feedback on his performance and help him to identify and rectify problems in his learning. This feedback, used to turn the test into a learning situation, can be provided at a number of levels. At the question level, the tutor may wish to provide a comment to each student who answers a question in a certain way. This might range from a simple message of encouragement for a correct response, to a detailed explanation of why a false answer was incorrect. Unless the tutor can devote a considerable amount of time to each student, it is usually impossible to carry out this sort of post-mortem analysis without some assistance from a CML system. If the test is already being scored by a computer, then it is a simple matter to arrange for suitable comments to be associated with each response to each question in the test, and for the appropriate comments to be printed out for each student. The student's score on particular parts of the test or his overall score can similarly be used to select a suitable message on his performance, and at a higher level, his performance can be combined with other information stored about him, to give him feedback on his progress.

The presentation and level of detail of this feedback varies considerably in different CML systems. At one extreme it may be given in a coded form so that the student must consult a code book to find out what was meant; at the other extreme, the computer can be programmed to combine all the comments into a personalised letter to the student. The latter approach is much more acceptable to the student who, like his tutor, should not find the computer obtrusive. It is therefore likely to be more useful educationally; the student will read the feedback in the form of sentences or a letter, but will be disinclined to make the effort of looking up the meanings of codes. Whilst extolling this ideal situation, we should realise that practical considerations such as the size of the computer and the way in which it is used can restrict the facilities available. A considerable amount of computer storage is required if long diagnostic comments are held and associated with each possible response to many questions in many tests. The length of the comments may also be restricted by the ability of the system to print out the individual reports for each student. If the storage or the speed of printing are limited, then so must be the diagnostic comments.

Most CML systems attempt to provide diagnostic feedback as quickly as possible to conform with the established view that if feedback is to be effective then it must be immediate. However the situation is more complex and it is arguable that some students may learn better if their feedback is delayed. For example, a student who is wrong and dogmatic about it may need time to come to terms with his errors. This may be one of the factors considered in tailoring courses to the needs and preferences of individual students, which is discussed later.

Test Analysis[†]

Writing good test items is difficult. Combining individual items to form a test which is both valid in that it measures the right things in the right way, and reliable so that the examiner can have some faith in the results he obtains, is more complex. These problems are not confined to MCQ objective tests but also beset subjective, short answer and essay-type tests; the difference is that for objective tests there are some standard ways of analysing the results to determine how reliable and valid the test has been. It is not the aim of this section to provide a full description of the various methods by which tests can be analysed, but rather to indicate how the computer can help in the process. The Bibliography at the end of the book contains several references to other texts which provide more comprehensive treatments of the topic. A test administered to a group of students yields information not only about the students, but also about the course and about the test itself. The results can be used to help the students with their learning difficulties, the tutor improve the course, and the examiner improve the tests. Alas this detailed analysis of the test involves a considerable amount of arithmetic and requires so much effort that it is usually only carried out by the most dedicated, or those who are forced to do so. A major benefit of CML test-marking procedures is that, since the results are already stored in the computer, these analyses can be carried out accurately and without any extra effort on the part of the teacher.

The Test as a Whole

The analyses can be divided into two parts, those which are concerned with the performance of the test as a whole and those which describe each individual question. First let us consider the test as a whole. The distribution of the scores for a group of students is perhaps the easiest of the statistics to obtain, certainly if the arithmetic is being done by hand or with a small calculator. A histogram can show the average and peak score, and the distribution about the mean. This gives a good indication of the test's ability to separate out good and bad students. The shape of the histogram is important. Often in educational testing, the aim is to place the students in some order of ability. This calls for tests which compare each student with his peers or some norm. Norm-referenced tests[†] typically have a bell-shaped or normal distribution and a wide spread of scores so that individual students are separated as much as possible. In diagnostic testing and in training, the purpose is to ascertain whether the student has understood a certain part of the course or can carry out a given task. Then, criterion-referenced tests,[†] which check the student's mastery of specific objectives, should be used and a different distribution may be expected. The shapes of these two curves are shown in Figure 4.5.

Figure 4.5: Distribution of Scores

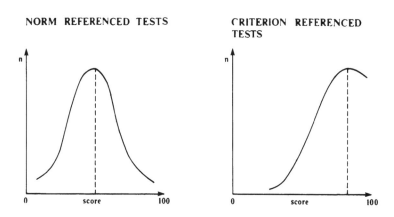

The shape of the distribution curve is particularly important for a Norm-referenced subjective test in which different batches of answer scripts have been marked by different examiners. Since the test is subjective, each examiner will put his own interpretation on the marking schedule and mark slightly differently from his colleagues. All the marks must then be moderated, that is, adjusted to impose a uniform, equitable standard. The adjustment may involve moving the mean score, adjusting the spread of the scores, or more usually both. This moderation to a prespecified mean and standard deviation is an obvious task for a CML testing system.

Various statistical techniques can be used to provide a measure of the reliability of the test and hence an indication of how accurate it is in assessing students. Most of these provide an intangible numerical value; the more reliable the test then the larger the value. One technique however, gives a value which the teacher can relate directly to his test. The Skurnick-Nuttal Measuremeter[†] indicates the number of grades into which the students could be divided by the test, with a probability of 0.95 that each student would be either given the correct grade, the one above it or the one below. For example, if a test gave a Skurnick-Nuttal Measuremeter value of 5, then it would be reasonable to divide the students into 5 grades, say A to E, so that a student given grade B would probably have a correct grade of A, B or C. It is a salutary experience to analyse a seemingly good test, on which the students would normally be graded from A+ to E− and discover that its excellence is an illusion − that seven distinct grades are all that can be expected.

Analysis of Individual Questions

Two useful statistics, the facility value[†] and the discrimination index,[†] can be calculated for each of the questions in the test. The facility value,[†] as its name implies, is a measure of how hard or easy the question was; the discrimination index is an indication of its ability to discriminate between 'good' and 'bad' students. Clearly, a question which is impossibly hard or absurdly easy, so that all the students get it wrong or get it right, contributes nothing to a norm-referenced test which is intended to separate students of different abilities. However, in a criterion-referenced test, a question which can be answered correctly by all the candidates who have mastered a given objective may be quite appropriate. The discriminating power of a question should be high, showing that it was answered correctly by the most able students, but that the less able students answered it incorrectly. Alas, if the question is badly phrased then its power to discriminate can be drastically reduced or even reversed, so that the good students fare badly on the item.[†] In this case the question actually detracts from the overall effectiveness of the test. Additional statistics for multiple choice questions can highlight distractors, that is alternative false answers, which have failed to seduce their fair share of weak candidates. Again, for some uses this may be a drawback, while for others, such as in criterion-referenced testing, it may show only that the particular objective has been mastered.

More sophisticated analyses of the test as a whole may show up common patterns of incorrect answers, indicating problem areas in the course. Thus, intelligent examination of all the various analyses can give considerable insight into the performance of the text and of the course.

It also affords the possibility of improving the performance of the test — after the students have taken it. Figure 4.6 shows the procedure which can be adopted with a CML test-marking and analysis system.

The test is marked and the results are analysed by the computer. The examiner is then given the opportunity of checking that the test has performed in the way he intended. Any questions that have proved too hard or too easy, or that behaved in a peculiar way, can be identified. If he wishes, the examiner can then change the marking scheme to ignore, or give less weight to, poor questions and use the computer to re-mark the entire test. Only when he is satisfied, are the marks published and the records updated. Clearly, the effort required to carry out this repeated marking and analysis would be impractical without the aid of the CML system.

Item Banking[†] and Test Construction

Having devised techniques to help with the marking of tests and to analyse the results, the next logical step is to use the computer to assist in the setting of tests. This involves setting up some means of storing a set of questions in the computer and then specifying rules which the machine can follow to make up a test from the available questions. The computer can help to construct a number of different tests with the same characteristics so that students can be re-tested if a section of the course is repeated, or so that equivalent tests can be given to different groups of students without compromising the questions. A systematic approach to course design requires that the objectives of the course are clearly defined. At a later stage in the course the student may be assessed, using questions which are closely related to the original objectives. The concept of testing to objectives allows the objectives to be defined by the questions which are to be used for assessment. The students can then be given a list of a very large number of questions which they might be asked in the examination. They have the choice of understanding the material in the course, in which case they will be able to answer the questions, or of memorising the answers to all the questions, in which case they will probably understand the material in the process. Such an approach to course assessment could be practicable with computer aided test construction.

Item Banking

The first task is to build up a file of questions, called an item bank, in the computer. Three things may be stored about each question. First, there must be some description of the item, including the subject

Figure 4.6: CML Marking Process

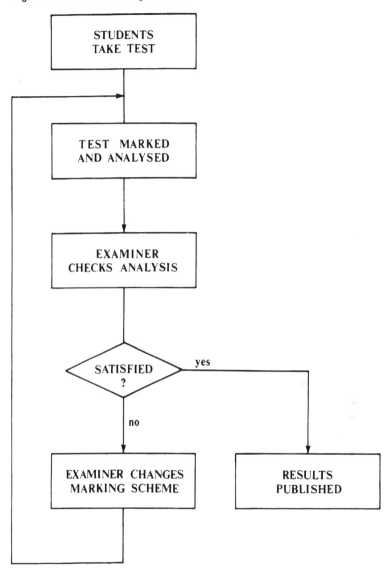

matter, the level of difficulty and the sort of knowledge which it intended to test. Then there may be the text of the question itself. This can present problems because the output printers commonly found on general purpose computers can print out numbers, letters and some symbols such as parentheses, commas, semicolons etc, but cannot usually deal with subscripts and superscripts, Greek letters, integral signs and other special symbols that may be used. Neither are they very good at printing complex diagrams or maps. If these are to be stored then they must be coded into large sets of numbers which adds to the storage required. This is the second problem. If an item bank is to be useful, then it must contain a large number of questions, and the computing resources needed to store the text of all the questions can be considerable.

Finally, the item bank should contain information about the performance of the question on each occasion it was used. Most of the statistics which are used to describe the performance of an item are only accurate in the context in which they were obtained. In other words, the facility value and index of discrimination obtained depend on the students taking the test and on the other questions in the test. One relatively new technique, the Rasch Method,[†] has overcome this difficulty for simple items which can be marked either right or wrong, and permits an analysis of the question which is largely independent of the context in which it was used. Unfortunately, the method is still being developed for the more complex scoring methods discussed above, for example questions using variable scoring and confidence levels. Under certain conditions, when the question is used repeatedly in the same test or when the student population taking the test can be assumed to remain constant from test to test, then the item statistics from each application of the test can be combined. This situation is quite common for the criterion-referenced items used in diagnostic testing, particularly in training environments.

From the collection, or file of stored questions, the computer can then be used to help in the construction of a test, or tests, with given characteristics of the questions to be selected from the file. The rules will determine the subject area or areas and the types of questions that are required. They may also indicate the sort of facility values and indices of discrimination that are needed and specify that recently used questions should not be included. From these rules, the computer can be programmed to extract a sufficient number of suitable questions and to predict the final characteristics of the test. The examiner can now decide whether the test is satisfactory; if it is not, then he can modify the rules and ask for another attempt. Perhaps he will reject some of the selected questions and request alternatives. This partnership between man and computer can be used to produce good and predictable tests, quickly and with less effort than by purely manual methods.

Test Construction

Thus far, the new test consists only of a list of question numbers. It must still be turned into a printed question paper that the student can use. In sophisticated systems this process too may be automated. However, the problems of storing and printing the text of test items has led some users to develop simpler systems in which only a description of the item with details of its past use are stored; the actual text of the item is held in printed form, perhaps in a filing cabinet. As the test is built up, a copy of each question is taken from the cabinet and photocopied. Although this requires more manual effort, it may well be more flexible and cost-effective.

A by-product of the test construction is a marking scheme for the test marking part of the CML system for when the test is used. Thus the four aspects of assessment, marking, analysis, item banking and test construction, are linked in the cycle shown in Figure 4.7.

Figure 4.7: CML Assessment Cycle

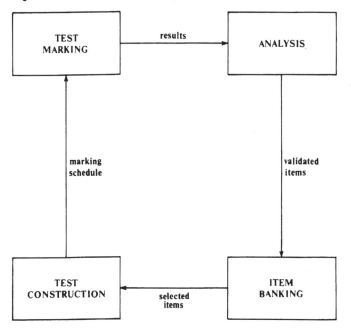

Routing†

The concept of using the computer to guide students through structured course materials is based on the assumption that the majority of students should follow one of a small number of paths. The rules governing the optimal path that should be followed by a particular student can then be prespecified by the tutor and subsequently interpreted by the CML system. At this point, the discourse may be interrupted by the educational psychologist who points out, quite correctly, that since we do not fully understand how students learn, it is impossible to lay down rules as to which is the best route through any course. This is a valid criticism of a system which attempts to prescribe and enforce a best route through the materials for all students. However, it can be argued that it is possible to provide useful guidance for most of the students, for most of the time. This can then cater for most of the routing decisions that would otherwise be taken by the tutor and allow him more time to concentrate on the minority of students who are in need of intelligent, as opposed to routine, help. The CML system is used to support the tutor, not to replace him.

The early CML systems assumed that the course was broken into a number of individual modules, each with well defined prerequisites and objectives, so that there was a well defined structure. If a student failed to master the objectives of a given module then he could automatically be told to repeat the module, or be directed to some remedial work. At each stage, his results on the post-test, possibly combined with previous test results, could be used to determine the next module in the sequence. This works acceptably in subjects where the course can be highly structured or where the students are amenable to being told what to do next. Mathematics and science teaching at secondary level and some kinds of industrial training are examples of this kind of environment. But if a CML system is to be used effectively outside these rather restricted limits, then it must also be free of any specific content and context. In other words, it should not be tied to a particular subject area or to a particular teaching and learning style. Thus while in some cases it may be appropriate to direct the student authoritatively from one learning task to the next, in others the CML system should adopt a softer advisory style. The students may prefer to study one module at a time, or wish to take the modules in groups. Others may flit from one module to another in what may seem to an outside observer a random manner. Where these study styles are educationally desirable then the CML system should be able to accept them.

There are many factors governing the choice of a next module. First of course, there is the knowledge, held within the CML system of the student's performance on various tests. This provides evidence of his mastery, or lack of it, of previous objectives which may be prerequisites for subsequent modules. Then there are the students' preferences for certain paths or for certain kinds of teaching and learning. Finally, the process should take into account the tutor's knowledge. Both the student and his tutor should be able to participate in the decision making, and to overrule the CML system if they want to. It is very easy for the student — and for the tutor too — to assume that the advice given by the computer is somehow better than that given by a teacher, and is irrefutable. Not so. The rules governing the routing decisions can be made as complex as the system and the tutor's ingenuity will allow, but the rules are still specified by the tutor or the course designer, embodying his knowledge and wisdom of how he would advise a student under those circumstances.

Record Keeping

In order to guide students effectively and to provide useful information to tutors and students, the CML system must maintain records, about the students' performance and progress, about the performance of the course and the tests involved — and perhaps about the teachers as well. The information stored relates to the students' scores on each test, to the modules they are currently studying, and to those they have completed. It may also include background information about their learning preferences, aspirations and problems, and comments made about them by the tutor. For each of the tests within the computer managed courses, the system may store statistics on overall performance and on each question.

Problems of Privacy

The problems of record keeping are not technological — computers are well able to store and process large quantities of data — but sociological. Many people are uneasy, and sometimes with good cause, about personal information stored in computer systems. Student records[†] are not a recent innovation. Teachers have long kept notes of their students' performance and progress, and usually in record books or index cards that may be less accurate and probably less secure than data stored in a well engineered computer system. However, the computer presents a more visible threat to privacy and so concern has focused on its use.

In legislation enacted in many countries and in codes of good practice promulgated in others, a number of principles have been held to describe an individual's right to privacy. Firstly, the existence of a student record system should not be kept secret, and the students concerned should be able to find out what information is kept about them. Secondly, they should be able to challenge any data that they believe is inaccurate, and any errors should be corrected. Finally, they must be assured that the information held about them will only be used for educational purposes and will not be divulged to people other than their teachers, course director and so on, without their express permission. These restrictions are, on superficial examination, very reasonable, but they do in reality make two, possibly unjustified, assumptions. Firstly, there is the assumption that the information held about the student, his performance and progress is in some way the personal property of the student, and secondly, that the student is the person who should be responsible for saying how it shall be used. We have already seen that the student records reflect, not only on the student himself, but also on the course that he is studying and on his teachers. Particularly in the case of younger students, they may also contain subjective comments about his home background, in which case they could yield information about the child's parents or guardian. The ownership of the data is then highly questionable, and it is not at all clear as to who can, or should, decide on reasonable uses. In some extreme cases, perhaps a discussion on the quality of teaching, the motives of teachers can conflict with those of parents.

This should not be taken as a prophecy of doom for record keeping in CML systems, but as a warning. The introduction of computer based student records should be preceded by discussions with all the parties involved and accompanied by adequate safeguards to ensure privacy. This is especially important where subjective or emotive comments about the students are to be stored.

Reporting

To manage his teaching or training effectively, the tutor needs information about his students' performance and progress. The student also needs feedback to manage his own learning. Thus the CML system must provide reports, based on the stored records, to all those involved in the teaching and learning process. These reports must be accurate, up to date, and most important, provide the appropriate information in the appropriate format. The student's report will include detailed feedback which is not needed by his tutor who is interested in broader indications of progress. More summarised information is required by the course director and higher levels of management. As in the case of computer generated feedback to students, discussed above, there are many possible variations in the presentation of this information — it may be printed out as a short essay in a series of selected paragraphs, in a more concise abbreviated form, or in extreme cases, as codes which must be interpreted. As a general rule, the less frequently the user receives the report, the closer to written prose must be the contents. So, while the student receives a report that resembles a personal letter giving him feedback and advice, the same information may be encoded, perhaps using mnemonic codes, in the report to his tutor.

An extension of reporting on students' achievements is to include reports on students' lack of progress. Given a knowledge of the students registered on a course and details of a reasonable rate of progress, the CML system can be programmed to indicate those students who are falling behind or who have omitted mandatory parts of the course. This enables the teacher to work on a principle of management by exception and concentrate on those of his students who have problems.

A CML system can also be used to produce reports on the performance of the courses which it manages, the diagnostic tests and examinations in those courses, and on the past and predicted demands on resources. For example, the system could print a report for a laboratory technician giving details of the apparatus required for the next practical lesson, or give a warning that an excessive number of students were converging on a part of the course where resources were limited. These reports can be used by the education or training organisation to improve the quality of courses and to anticipate problems while there is still time to find a solution.

Extensions to CML Systems

The view of a supportive computer managed learning system working unobtrusively in the background to assist the teacher and his students by assuming some of the routine tasks in education and training, lends itself to extensions beyond the immediate teaching and learning process, or beyond the middle portion of the range of information described in Chapter 1. One of the problems of CML is that of collecting the basic data about the student's activities. Clearly, if some of these activities are themselves centred on the computer, then the basic data can be passed across to the CML system automatically. Thus if CAL packages are used in a computer managed course, the packages can provide information directly into the CML records.

Another extension, more sensitive in respect of privacy, is the linking of a computer based library circulation system with CML. It might be thought that a great deal of information could be gleaned about a student's progress from an intelligent examination of the books or other resources he has borrowed from the library, where these can be related to particular parts of the course. However this method of inferring what the student is doing only works if he actually borrows the materials from the library and then uses them. It provides no trace of browsing activities or his use of other resources which are not controlled in this way, and false information for materials which are borrowed but not used.

Student Record Systems

At the other end of the range, the records kept by the CML system can be processed by the computer to provide input to existing student record systems. Here again, there is no real boundary between the sort of records used by the teaching staff and those required by high-level administrators, such as Government departments, who are interested only in overall student numbers, pass rates, subjects studied and the like. Indeed some sophisticated CML systems are being extended to carry out such functions and so provide a single integrated system that can be used at all levels. While this may sound very Orwellian and menacing, it offers considerable savings in the effort needed to process educational information, and in the number of errors that may be made in transferring information from one stage to the next. In order to justify such a system it must be firmly and clearly directed towards the benefit of the students.

Careers Counselling

Further extensions to this idea of an integrated educational information system are obvious. The process of guiding the student through a modular course has been described in terms of decision making by applying prespecified rules to what is known about the student. Thus the system can handle routine decisions for the majority of cases. This is very similar to the process of careers counselling which uses much the same basic student information, but a different set of rules to advise the student on possible career opportunities. The student's aspirations for the future may be relevant to the courses or learning paths he should follow, and hence these two aspects interact as shown in Figure 4.8.

This shows the two cycles, learning and careers counselling, as separate systems — in practice they may well be two different applications of the same general purpose system running side by side, and sharing the same set of records. There are other ways in which the ubiquitous CML system and its student records can be extended to support other activities associated with education and training — if the teachers and trainers wish it. The limits of its usefulness are not, in general, technological, but the extent to which teachers, counsellors and administrators can identify and define their routine management tasks.

Figure 4.8: The Interaction Between Learning and Counselling in a CML Environment

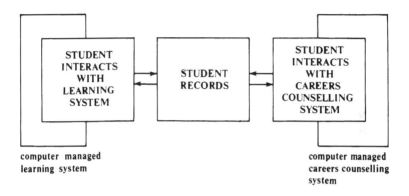

computer managed
learning system

computer managed
careers counselling
system

Education, Training and Management

The preceding description of facilities that can be provided by computer managed learning systems makes an impressive catalogue. We should now consider the impact that CML can or should make on education and training. An important point is that CML offers solutions to management problems, and not directly to educational problems. Its effect is to free the teacher from some of the constraints which have previously prevented him from developing the course that, educationally, he might like to use. When planning a new course, or modifying an existing one, the teacher, either consciously or unconsciously, will restrict his options to those he knows are practicable. For example, if faced with a highly unfavourable staff-student ratio he will tend to think in terms of a lock step, lecture based course, which will reduce the management required to a tolerable level: he will reject continual diagnostic testing because it will take up too much time; in designing a distance learning[†] course he will try to simplify the course structure and minimise the number of occasions on which the student needs to consult his tutor, because of the problems of communication. In a teaching or training environment supported by a CML system these restrictions are relaxed and some otherwise labour-intensive forms of teaching become possible — if the teacher wants to use them. He should not feel obliged to use all the CML facilities just because they are there, any more than he should feel obliged to use the overhead projector or closed-circuit television in every lesson. So, CML will not solve his problems of how to structure a student-centred course, or how to build effective diagnostic tests. Indeed, by reducing the problems of management, the educational problems may become more apparent. Once he has devised an educationally satisfactory course, then the CML system will help him to run it.

Ideally, the CML system should be value free, that is, neither tied to specific curriculum materials nor to a specific style of teaching and learning. In practice this is rarely attained. Nevertheless the systems which are available have proved to be effective and useful aids in the management of teaching and training.

Resource Management[†]

Related to the use of the computer as an educational manager is the application of the computer to the administrative processes of the institution. One of the most complex administrative problems in a school or university department, is the production of an efficient time-table which will make the best use of the available resources, matching teachers, rooms, laboratories and the like to the students and the combinations of subjects they are studying. It can be argued that the time-table is as important as the curriculum; while the curriculum is a statement of aims, it is the timetable which maps these into a coherent and practicable deployment of the institution's staff, teaching a variety of subjects to suitable sized groups of students, for given periods of time in suitable teaching spaces. Similar problems, although on a smaller scale, are encountered in the preparation of examination timetables. Training establishments vary considerably in the complexity of their scheduling tasks. Small training organisations with few courses operating at regular intervals have very little difficulty in arranging their timetables, but larger establishments, with many students, with courses running in parallel, competing for scarce resources, and operating on different cycles and starting dates, may be faced with a very difficult problem.

Computer assisted timetabling or scheduling can help the time-tabler — at least to devise the basic framework for the timetable. The production of the timetable is an iterative process, in other words the timetabler will start by fixing various resources and groups that are likely, from experience, to be troublesome, and add in other groups until he comes to an impasse or a solution. Then, by altering some parts of the timetable, he can try to improve, or complete the solution. Sometimes it is not possible to construct a timetable which fulfils the initial requirements of the institution and so the requirements must be relaxed to enable a compromise solution to be found. Much of this repetitive, trial and error process can be handled by the computer, leaving the timetabler free to exercise his inspiration and add his experience of changes which may improve the final solution.

While computer assisted timetabling is not a panacea, it does offer a number of advantages including a higher overall fit with fewer compromises, a good control of the spread of subjects over the teaching week and in consequence, a better deployment of teachers and their free time. Although in the early stages of its use, very little time may be saved, because the users must become familiar with the system and because the input data must be prepared carefully, on subsequent occasions the technique can be cost-effective and make it feasible to experiment with different arrangements as part of the institution's planning process. Where the initial requirements must be changed to obtain a compromise solution, the problem areas can be highlighted and weaknesses in the institution's structure can be identified. Finally, when the master schedule has been fixed, it is an easy matter to obtain multiple copies of different parts of the timetable for each teacher, student and resource.

Timetabling is usually associated only with matching students to teachers and rooms, rather than with a consideration of other resources such as books, visual aids or laboratory equipment. But these items must also be available in suitable quantities and some must be scheduled. The administrator must therefore maintain financial and inventory control and provide information to the institution about what is available generally, and within the institution itself. Here again, the computer can be used to help the teacher and the educational or training administrator, by keeping records of the resources, where they are kept, the rate at which they are being consumed if appropriate, and their cost. The computer system can be set up to provide reports for the teachers and administrators on the availability of resources and to prompt them to re-order when stocks get low. These applications are not unique to education or training but are similar to the financial and stock control procedures in commerce and industry.

5 INFORMATICS AND EDUCATION

The Priesthood

The earliest recognisable computers emerged from research laboratories in the late 1940s; twenty-five years later they were already in use in a myriad of applications and, helped by repeated advances in electronics technology, they are now spreading even faster. Futurologists have remarked that the time required for a new technology to establish itself becomes less and less as technology in general advances. The rate of change also quickens with time, giving an exponential growth. In the case of computers, the timespan between their initial development and their introduction in numbers sufficient to cause a significant impact on society – about twenty-five years – is important. Previously, each generation of children has grown up with the technologies it uses and has had time to become accustomed to them. Now, we find ourselves making wide-scale use of something which is so new that it has not been included in most peoples' basic education. Further, most people only see a small part of a computer based system, usually the output from it in the form of a bank statement or gas bill. Perhaps it is not so surprising that, in these circumstances, a powerful mystique has grown up to surround computers and their operation. The aura of mystery, an excellent example of the adage that 'any sufficiently advanced technology is indistinguishable from magic', was perpetuated by a high priesthood who were thought of as the only beings who could understand these marvellous machines. The computer, almost a demigod, was paradoxically regarded as infallible by the general populace, yet culpable for any errors or failings which might occur in the systems they supported. A statement of account printed by the computer was not to be questioned – 'the computer says so, so it must be right', while any problems could be blamed on it – 'we regret that the computer made a mistake', or 'we cannot do that any more because the computer will not allow it'.

These unfortunate attitudes arose because relatively few people understood what computers could and could not do; computers were not a part of their general education. Although, as we shall see, this problem is now being tackled and, at least partially, overcome, it is still a common misconception that an in-depth knowledge of computers, their operation, and how to program them, is an essential prerequisite to using them and understanding their strengths and weaknesses. This is not true. Computing has come a long way from the early experimental

76

machines in university laboratories and now a good analogy can be drawn with the motor car — you can be a good driver without knowing how to design a car or how it works internally, and you can be a good passenger and enjoy the benefits of motor travel without knowing how to drive. This also applies to the use of computers in education and training. Its effective use depends on the educational context in which it is used rather than on the teacher having an empathy for it or knowing how to work it. This said, there is nevertheless a relationship between the study of computers and the use of computers in education and training.

Computer Awareness

As the use of computers grew, there was a concern among some teachers about society's lack of knowledge of computing, and a feeling that this should be rectified by including some computing in the secondary school curriculum. This of course posed another problem because very few of the teachers themselves knew much about the subject and hence it was envisaged that in-service courses in computing would also have to be provided.

Two assumptions, both of them very questionable, were made; first that computing is essentially related to mathematics and physics, and second, that in order to gain some appreciation of the subject the student must learn about the internal workings of computers and how to write programs for them. The first assumption can be dismissed. The association with mathematics and physics is purely historical and arises from the early uses of computers as machines for carrying out lengthy numerical calculations. Hopefully the earlier examples of CAL and CML used in divers subject areas will have dispelled any misconception that the computer cannot help to solve problems in other science subjects, and in non-scientific subjects such as history and geography, and can also be used for non-numerical problems such as extracting relevant pieces of information from a mass of data.

The computer is primarily a machine for storing and manipulating — processing — information. It can do this very quickly and accurately which gives it a big advantage over people for some applications. The information it processes may be numerical, in which case it is acting as a calculating-machine, or it may be the text of a play, in which case it is acting as a literary or linguistic machine. It can process other kinds of information for other applications. So it is also very versatile and can be described as a general purpose machine.

The concept of a computer as a processor of information moves the focus of our attention away from the machine and its internal functioning to the information it works on and the effect of this on our use of information. Hence the use of the word 'informatics'[†] in the title of this chapter, meaning the study of information,[†] the way we manipulate it and use it. From this viewpoint, informatics seems more relevant as a way of helping people to understand the impact that computers have on their daily lives than an approach which takes them into the working of computers and writing programs. Of course there is a case for teaching a detailed knowledge of computers − computer science − just as there is a case for teaching pure mathematics or geology, but these are all subjects to be studied by groups of students who want to specialise in that particular area, not topics for all students.

We should aim to provide our students with sufficient knowledge of computers and informatics so that they can make general and social inferences on the basis of what they see, hear and encounter themselves, of computers. Earlier in this chapter we started to draw an analogy between our general awareness of motor cars and of computers. Most of us know quite a lot about cars in terms of their general appearance (a box with seats for between two and six people, with a wheel at each corner and some sort of motor to propel it), what they do (transport their occupants along roads at an average speed of between 40 and 100 kilometres per hour), what advantages they have over other forms of transport (personal, private and relatively comfortable) and what their disadvantages are (expensive, potentially lethal, and tiresome in large numbers − particularly in traffic jams). We acquire this knowledge at an early age because, for most people, motor cars are part of everyday life. We learn what it is like to ride in a car, how to behave near them as a pedestrian (although it is dangerous to stand in front of them when they are moving, stationary cars are relatively harmless) and what impact they have on the quality of life (motorways are useful to the long-distance traveller but unpleasant to live beside). Some people learn how to drive cars and so become more intimately concerned with their use, but only a very few plumb the inner mysteries and come to understand their detailed workings. For the majority a superficial knowledge of the mechanics is sufficient for them to be generally aware of motor cars, their potential and their limitations, and their impact on everyday life.

We should try to provide a similar kind of background knowledge about computers so that we and our students appreciate what computers can and cannot do, what advantages they have over other ways of doing the same jobs, and what their disadvantages are. Properly used, the computer can make life easier and make possible what would otherwise be impractical. Badly used, it is at best a trivial distraction to the job in hand; at worst, a malevolent machine that prevents its users from doing their job properly. Unfortunately, for the first two decades of computer development, they were not a part of everyday life and, with a few exceptions, teachers were unfamiliar with them. Thus, an awareness of computers, their possibilities and their limitations developed but slowly.

Controlling How Computers Process Information

The computer[†] is essentially an information-processing machine. Inside the computer, small pieces of information can be moved around, and combined or compared with other pieces very rapidly and accurately. The way in which the computer manipulates the information is controlled by a set of instructions which is called a program. Its prime advantage over other means of processing information is the speed and repeatability with which it can move, compare and combine the individual pieces. Unlike a human being, it does not tire and will continue to carry out its instructions precisely. The key to understanding its greatest disadvantage lies in the phrase 'carry out its instructions precisely'. The computer must be given a set of instructions which specify in great and exact detail what it is to do. Thus, one set of instructions, or program,[†] could be used to enable the computer to solve a particular kind of equation, while another program would instruct it to simulate a patient for a CAL package. For any other than the simplest tasks, the computer programs are large and quite complicated. In general they are written by people, and are therefore likely to contain some errors. A discussion of errors in computer programs and how to avoid them is a subject in its own right; all we need to be aware of is that errors can and almost always do exist inside large computer programs, and that their effect is to make the computer do something other than what was intended. Two common kinds of errors are where an incorrect instruction is given or where an instruction or group of instructions is omitted at some point in the sequence.

As an example of a simple program, the following set of instructions might be given to a child on how to boil an egg.

1.   Put some water in a saucepan.
2.   Put in an unbroken egg.
3.   Boil for three and a half minutes.
4.   Remove egg.

In a computer program, each of these four steps would be expanded into a series of smaller steps. Step one might become:

1.1   Get saucepan from cupboard.

1.2   Carry saucepan to cold water tap.

1.3   Turn on tap and add 50ml of water.

1.4   If the water in the pan is 5cm deep (diameter of an egg) then go on to step 1.5, otherwise repeat step 1.3.

Some of these steps may need further expansion and an error in any one of them could result in an incorrect program — and an unacceptable boiled egg. An important difference between the computer program and even an inexperienced child is that the child will accept incomplete instructions and fill in the gaps from its background knowledge; the computer generally will not. At higher and more sophisticated levels of problem solving, the human being can fill less obvious gaps by using intuition. This is very difficult to program into a computer. We should note that these inaccuracies and omissions are a direct consequence of human error, not the computer's error; the computer will do exactly as it is instructed — even if the instructions are wrong.

Living with Computers

Our study of computer awareness should also include living with computers, the effects they have on everyday life and their future social impact. Although, given their reliability and high speed of operation, it should be possible to design computer based systems which are fast and flexible so that they can help us by providing a better service in a wide variety of situations, in practice users have found that the computer based system is often less personal and less flexible than the alternative which is centred on people. The solution, as illustrated in the application of computers to education and training by this text, is not rejection but an appropriate use of the technology based on an awareness of what computers can and cannot do. Experience is a powerful form of education and so encounters with computers in everyday situations can help us and our students learn how to live with them. We come across computers in a great variety of environments from bank accounts to airline reservation systems — and in education and training too. So, without actually teaching our students about computers they can learn what it is like to work with them by using them as part of their studies in other subjects. To a certain extent then, it behoves us to ensure that our use of CAL and CML does make appropriate and effective use of this technology.

While the majority acquire an awareness of computers there is of course a need for a number of computing specialists who will be responsible for designing, building and operating computer based systems on behalf of the users. The greater part of this text is concerned with presenting computer assisted and computer managed learning to the teacher and trainer, rather than to the specialist in computing. From time to time in the development and use of CAL and CML there will be problems which properly fall within the competence of the specialist either as a consultant or as an integral part of the project team. Some of these issues, such as the provision of computing facilities and the methods of writing CAL programs are discussed briefly in the following chapter on 'Technological Aspects'.

Solving Problems

In the preceding section we saw how the use of computers in education and training can help students (and teachers) to become more familiar with them. There is also a benefit to education from the specialist study of computer science, particularly from the skill of problem-solving with the aid of a computer. The simple example of a set of instructions on how to boil an egg showed how an apparently straightforward task relied on a considerable amount of experience and initiative from the child carrying out the instructions. Knowing that the water in the saucepan was required for boiling an egg, the child could select a suitable sized pan and fill it to the required depth without making a conscious allowance for its diameter (a larger pan needs more water). Even if the child had never filled a saucepan with water before it might do it by extending its experience of filling a toy bucket, and so on. A computer program to carry out the same task must be quite explicit and show all the substeps in the process. It may be that some previous program still held in the computer can be used to provide the details. Then the egg program need only state, for example, using program 'fillpan' put enough water in a saucepan to cover an egg. But, at some time, now or in the past, the complete and exact sequence of instructions on how to select and fill the pan with the appropriate quantity of water must be specified for the computer.

Although on first encounter, it might appear that this rigour is an unnecessary barrier to using the computer, it is part of a general discipline of systematic problem solving which is applicable beyond the tasks of writing computer programs. The systematic approach begins with a formal definition of the problem which includes the conditions under which it is to be solved. In this case the problem is to cook an egg by boiling it until the white is set but the yolk is still liquid. The next stage is to design a solution to the problem. The solution for our task of cooking an egg is well known; the egg must be immersed in boiling water for three and a half minutes with an acceptable error of plus or minus fifteen seconds. The length of time may need to be increased slightly for very large or very fresh eggs. Armed with a design, we must now construct the solution and test it. Perhaps the solution is something we do ourselves — a particular course of action — or, like a computer program, it may be something that must be made. Either way it must be checked under different conditions to ensure that it is a satisfactory, accurate and complete solution to the original problem. It is conceivable that the colour of the egg, or its shape or the time of day could affect the time required to cook it. The testing process should be carried out in such a way as to show up any possible errors, which can then be corrected.

The use of computers for problem solving teaches this discipline by imposition, but it then usefully spills over into other applications. Much of the process of using computers to solve problems revolves around the organisation of pieces of information and the way in which these are to be moved around and combined inside the computer. The systems approach to problem solving is concerned with the way that information about the problem is marshalled and the necessary solution is produced.

Computer assisted learning can thus be used to help teach a systematic approach to problem solving. In the revelatory form of CAL described in Chapter 2, the student works with a model of some real-life situation which is gradually revealed to him through a sequence of answers to questions posed by him and demonstrations of the model's behaviour under different circumstances. The efficiency of this process from the student's point of view depends on the investigative strategy that he adopts. A systematic approach is more likely to yield the required information quickly than a haphazard one. It is also likely to provide more effective learning of the subject material, although this is not always true.

Conjectural CAL is more explicit in its aim of teaching problem-solving. The student is asked to use the computer to form and test hypotheses which can be regarded as solutions of the behaviour of a given system or a computer model of it. Again, the student's strategy in organising his investigation and his approach to solving problems are central features of the learning.

Informatics and CAL

Teachers and instructors are problem solvers. Their problems are to teach various subjects to groups of students, and their solutions are in terms of lectures, learning packages and so on. Thus there is scope for these problem-solving techniques in teaching and indeed, under the name

Figure 5.1: A Systems Approach to Education and Training

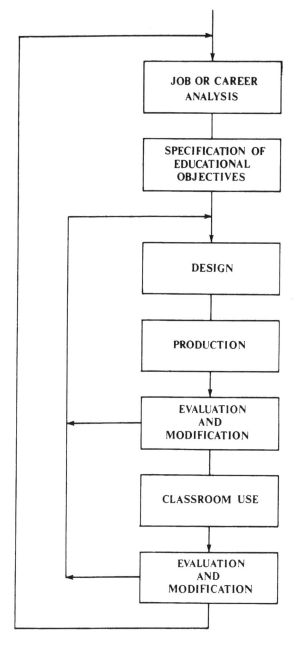

of a systems approach to training, they have been used in industry and the armed services for some time. In education, where there is less emphasis on cost-effectiveness and where the objectives are usually less easily defined, the systems approach has made less impact. The starting-point of this approach, shown in Figure 5.1, is an investigation of the environment for which the student is being educated or trained, and the consequent overall goals of the learning package.

From this study can come a detailed specification of the educational aims. The next stages are design and production of materials and these are followed by pilot trials and initial evaluation. The package is modified in the light of these experiences and then released for more wide-scale use. The evaluation of its performance in the classroom may result in further modification or be combined with a further study of how those students who have completed the course fare in their careers, and so influence the original specification of objectives. One valuable by-product of computer assisted learning is that it encourages a systematic problem-solving approach to learning by requiring teachers to specify their objectives clearly and to think about the design of the learning package. The CAL component of the package is the computer program which is itself bound to the same systematic method of production. (There is an obvious link here with the concept of programmed learning packages which are in effect, a sequence of instructions — a program — on learning a given topic.) Subsequently, the CAL program can provide some of the information that is necessary to validate it and evaluate its performance. The systematic approach to designing and building learning packages that is encouraged by CAL is not a magic formula for success, but it can be a great help in improving their efficacy.

6 TECHNOLOGICAL ASPECTS

The previous chapter examined what we should teach our students, and know ourselves about computers, as part of our general knowledge or awareness. We have repeatedly affirmed that no in-depth understanding of computers is required in order to use them as effective tools in education and training. However, we must have some superficial knowledge of the computing resources which are to support the educational methods and materials. The resources may be divided into the computers themselves, the terminals which are used to communicate with the computers and the CAL programs which determine how the computers operate.

The Computers

As we have seen, a computer[†] is essentially a machine for storing and manipulating information. The way in which it moves information about, and combines or compares small pieces of information inside itself is controlled by a set of instructions called a program. Different programs will instruct the computer to work in different ways, to process different kinds of information for different purposes. Computers, like many other commodities, come in a wide range of sizes with a great variety of special facilities – and with commensurate purchase and operating costs. In as much as most computers can be programmed for computer assisted learning applications, the CAL user has a potentially bewildering choice. At this superficial level, it is sufficient that the chosen machine can work with the number of terminals required for teaching and that it has sufficient storage capacity to keep all the CAL programs that are used and the student records that they may generate. Usually, and especially in the early stages of CAL development in an institution, there will be no choice of a computer because the existing facilities are the only ones available. If and when the CAL demand grows to justify a computer dedicated[†] to educational computing, it will be time to call upon computer specialists to advise on a detailed specification.

The Centralised Computer Centre

The kinds of computing facilities available do, however, influence the costs of teaching with CAL and the control that the teacher has over availability and so on. The bulk of computer facilities in educational institutions is usually provided by a large central computer which is shared by a number of users.[†] In practice this may be a large single computer or a number of connected computers, but usually it is arranged so that the user does not have to be aware of the precise arrangement, or configuration, because he sees only a simplified picture of the machine through his terminal. The speed of the computer enables it to do small pieces of work for each of the users in turn so quickly that each is unaware that other people are using the machine simultaneously. This is analogous to the way in which cine pictures, shown in rapid sequence give the illusion of continuous motion. The use of a central computer service is attractive to the CAL practitioner for a number of reasons. Firstly, it already exists, and so it avoids the necessity of acquiring and installing a large and expensive piece of equipment for the sole purpose of education or training. Because of the cost of a large computer, its purchase must be carefully considered and this can take a long time. Secondly, where a computer is shared, it is often possible to provide more comprehensive facilities than would be available in a smaller system. Thirdly, once installed, the computer may need a trained person to operate it and will certainly require a member of staff to become familiar with the facilities it provides. Where there is a central computer, these resources will already be available. Often the centre can provide much greater knowledge and support than would be possible in a small unit dedicated to computer based learning. Finally, as we shall see later, there are some economies of scale in using large computers so that CAL fills in the gaps left by other applications. This reduces the effective costs of using computer assisted and computer managed learning.

Dedicated Computer Facilities

The main disadvantage of using a large central computer is the lack of control that the CAL practitioner has over the machinery he needs to support his teaching. While in the early stages of development and use, computer assisted learning can fit in with other work on the computer, as it grows it may come into conflict with other users. A single user or small group of users may have very little influence over the scheduling of the computer, the times of day when it is working but assigned to other work or unavailable because of routine maintenance, and the existing schedule may not fit in with the times when the teachers would like their students to use CAL. Further, as CAL usage grows, the balance of facilities that are required may not match that which is available. These problems have caused some CAL projects to accept the overheads of installing and operating their own computer dedicated to CAL. These may vary in size from a machine which is only slightly more sophisticated than an elaborate desk-top calculator, to a computer capable of operating with sixty or more terminals at once. A few exceptional CAL systems have very large computers and can handle up to several thousand terminals simultaneously. However, to the user, most computers provide similar kinds of facilities and can be used for computer assisted learning; the differences are in the convenience of use, costs and control. The possible exception to the general rule that CAL can cohabit with other applications in a general purpose educational computer, is computer managed learning. CML systems can be used to store large quantities of information about the performance and progress of students working on different courses, and about the courses themselves. The amount of storage space needed in the computer to keep all this information conveniently available can be an embarrassment to a small educational computer centre, and the problem must be considered at an early stage in the development of a CML system.

Computing Facilities in Industry

Much of the previous section applies to training as well as to education, making suitable allowances for the different environments. In an educational institution, a central service may be provided by a large general purpose computer, but such provision is less common in industry where computers are installed and reserved for specific tasks. With the exception of the computer industry itself, research and development organisations and a few special applications such as in mail order companies and airlines, computer systems with many terminals suitable for CAL work are uncommon. Thus it is often difficult for a training department to find existing facilities that are suitable for their use. This makes it more attractive to think in terms of a dedicated CAL system, under the instructors' control. Because of the different fiscal natures of education and training organisations, the question of cost-effectiveness is likely to be more carefully examined in the latter.

Communications

In order that the student seated at his terminal can use the computer, there must be some means of communication between the terminal and the computer. Again this is a subject in its own right, but for the purposes of this discussion it is convenient to consider communications and the computer together, as machinery which is mainly hidden from the CAL user. Where a small computer is only able to work with a single terminal, then the two units will usually be physically close together and are often in the same box. The pieces of wire joining the two are not apparent and can be ignored. As the number of terminals increases, they are more likely to be dispersed around a classroom, a building, or perhaps over the whole educational campus or factory site. Where the distances are relatively short, say less than a few hundred metres, or the terminals are in constant use, then it is convenient to have each terminal permanently connected to the computer by a cable, much as a telephone is connected to a private switchboard. However, where terminals are to be used with a computer that is more than a few kilometres distant, then it is preferable to use the existing telephone network, and make (and pay for) the connection only when the terminal is in use.

The Terminals

The most usual, but not the only, way for a student to use a computer assisted learning program is by communicating with the computer through a terminal.[†] This incorporates some means for the student to send messages to the computer and for the computer to reply. Almost invariably the student uses a typewriter-like keyboard for his input to the computer and is restricted to sending messages consisting only of letters, digits and some special symbols. Because of the constraints which this imposes, a number of alternative means of input have been investigated, not only for CAL but also for other interactive computer applications. These range from the provision of extra keys which can be used to signify frequently used responses such as 'yes', 'no', 'help' and so on, to a means of positioning a pointer or cursor over the terminal display screen so that the student can indicate a particular part of the output. Some terminals incorporate a special touch-sensitive screen. This allows the student to indicate various words in the displayed text or a specific point on a diagram by touching the screen at that point.

Early terminals were developed from electric typewriters and teleprinters and displayed the computer output by printing it on a continuous roll of paper. They were noisy because of the continual impact of the type against the paper, and rather unreliable because of the large number of mechanical parts and precise adjustments needed. Fortunately, modern printing terminals[†] are quieter and more reliable. The advantage of a printing terminal is that it provides a permanent record of the CAL lesson so that the student can refer back to earlier passages and at the end of a session can take the record away with him.

An alternative to printing the output on paper is to display it on a screen similar to that used in a television set. Such terminals are called Visual Display Units (VDUs).[†] Because of its lack of moving parts these are silent and much more reliable than printing machines. Unfortunately, the size of the screen limits the amount of output that can be displayed at any one time and so it is difficult for the student to return to output that was produced earlier in the lesson and there is no permanent record for him to take away. Although it is possible to connect a printer to some VDUs to make a hard copy of the display, the copies are expensive and this limits their usefulness. Like printing terminals, most visual display units are restricted to a limited range of characters — letters, digits and some symbols. With some ingenuity simple diagrams can be composed of character patterns, using letter Is for vertical lines, dashes for horizontal lines and characters such as O * M W and X for degrees of shading, but complex figures are very difficult.

Graphics Terminals†

Where complex diagrams are required, the CAL user must turn to graphics terminals which can draw pictures, graphs, diagrams and so on, as a series of lines and line segments, as well as displaying text. Some of these are available with facilities for displaying shades of grey and different colours. All these features greatly widen the possibilities for presenting complex information in easily assimilable ways; alas, graphics terminals are inevitably more expensive than alphameric VDUs.

In general, computer assisted learning uses general purpose terminals which have been developed for other applications but which are broadly suitable for the kind of dialogue† between student and computer in a CAL environment. We have already seen that CAL is often only one component in a multi-media package and this has led to a number of projects which sought to develop a special purpose CAL terminal. This concept brings together a number of different media, all under the control of the student and the computer, at a single learning station. Existing alphameric and graphics terminals interpret the signals they receive from the computer as instructions to print specified characters or to draw lines in certain positions. It can be arranged that other distinct signals are instructions to manipulate other media, for example, to select and display a specified photographic slide or microfiche image, to play a sound recording on a tape-recorder, or to synthesise a verbal message to the student. Although their comprehensive facilities have an obvious attraction, the enthusiasm of the CAL community has been tempered by the high cost of such terminals and by the difficulties of using them effectively.

Interactive† or Batch Computing

Thus far there has been an implicit assumption that computer assisted learning requires students to use terminals in order to communicate with the computer. There is another, and for some applications a more convenient, means of access. The difference between interactive and batch computing[†] can be compared with the use of the telephone and postal systems. Interactive use through a terminal connected to the computer is analogous to using a telephone. The telephone is an appropriate means of communication if you want to hold a conversation with another person some distance away. The dialogue consists of a sequence of short messages, each dependent on what has gone before. If larger quantities of information are to be sent, there is little or no dependence on previous messages and time is not critical, then the postal system, equivalent in this analogy to batch use of the computer, may be more appropriate.

Interactive, terminal based CAL provides an immediacy of access and rapid, almost instant dialogue with the computer. The traditional belief that rapid feedback to students on the effect of their decisions is important in effective learning, has resulted in many CAL developments going hand in hand with the growth of interactive computing. However, as we have seen in previous chapters, for some CAL applications a batch method may be acceptable, or may even be preferable. In a batch environment, the student prepares his input away from the computer and writes it down on a form. This data[†] is then transcribed onto a suitable medium which can be read by the computer and takes its turn in a queue of programs or jobs waiting to be run. After it has been processed by the computer, the output is returned to the student. There is a delay inherent in batch operation due to the necessity of moving information from the student to the computer and back again. Depending on how this is organised and how the computer is used, this delay can range from several minutes to several days. Batch access offers two advantages. First, by avoiding the need for terminals and the lines which connect them to the computer it is cheaper than interactive CAL. Second, in applications where there is a large quantity of output from the computer it is preferable to have this printed at high speed by the special printer attached to the computer, rather than to have the student sitting at the terminal for a long time watching his output appear at perhaps thirty characters a second. So, where the student's dialogue with the computer is not really interactive or immediate, or where the quantity of output is large, a batch system should be considered. These conditions are found in many computer managed learning systems where the student's study cycle — the rate of exchange of information — is running on a timescale of hours or days rather than seconds or minutes, and the reports to the student and his teachers can be long.

The Programs

We have seen that, in order for the computer to carry out its tasks, it must be provided with sequences of instructions called programs which specify in precise detail all the many small steps that must be followed to obtain the desired result. Let us now consider how we can produce these programs effectively and reasonably cheaply. Given the complexity of most CAL programs it would, at first sight, appear that writing the necessary programs is an incredibly tedious task, and that writing programs that do not contain any errors is almost impossible. Fortunately there are tools that can be used to make this task considerably easier. The main tool is the programming language which helps in three ways. First, it provides prespecified sequences of instructions to carry out operations which are frequently used. Thus, instead of writing out all the individual steps needed to print a line of text on a terminal, the program author can use a special word such as 'write' followed by the message he wants printed. Second, it enables the author to write in a style which suits him rather than in a way constrained by the machine. Arithmetic expressions can be written so that they resemble mathematical notation or a tutorial CAL program can be constructed of a sequence of frames. Third, the programming language can supply various checks to reduce the possibility of errors. A great many programming languages[†] exist; some have been designed for specialist applications such as project management or computer assisted learning while others, with greater or lesser justification, claim to be of general purpose. A handful of the latter group, such as Algol, Fortran, Basic and Cobol, are in common use, and one or more of them is usually available for use with any particular computer. Among the tasks they can be used for is CAL — most of the CAL programs in existence are written in a general purpose programming language. Each language has its group of disciples who will argue long in support of their favourite and in condemnation of all others. In truth they are all like the curate's egg — good in parts; most can be used effectively for CAL work and the choice between them is usually constrained by availability, rather than made on relative merits.

A similar war of words rages between the protagonists of general purpose languages and those who favour languages designed specifically for CAL applications. These languages can simplify the task of writing CAL programs by including standard ways of carrying out standard operations, such as matching a student's response against a list of expected responses while allowing for certain kinds of errors, or adding the results of an assessment to the student's record. Although these languages are often less efficient in their use of computer resources and less flexible than general purpose languages (for example they may have only limited facilities for mathematical operations), their ease of use and educational orientation makes them attractive to teachers and instructors writing CAL packages.

One advantage generally claimed for programming languages is that programs written in such a language can be run on any computer for which the language is available. Thus, most computers can run programs written in Fortran or Basic and it would appear that a program written in one of these languages could be run without alteration on almost any computer. Unfortunately computer languages, like natural languages, have dialects and two dialects can differ so much that they might as well be two different languages. The use of a general purpose programming language is not a guarantee that the program can be transferred from one machine to another without alteration.

The programming language, whether a general purpose language or one designed specifically for CAL, is the author's point of contact with the computer — it is the one area of specialist knowledge that the author[†] must have. In some cases the teacher or instructor using CAL may produce the materials himself and so must learn how to program in a suitable language. Alternatively, the project may employ a programmer to do this work, or call on one of the staff from the computer centre. Programming is a very charismatic and addictive occupation, and once introduced to the delights of instructing the computer many users, including teachers, find it irresistibly attractive. The function of a teacher is to instruct his students — not the computer. Writing good programs is a very demanding occupation requiring a thorough knowledge of the language and an empathy with the machine.

Reliability and Resilience

Reliability and resilience are of paramount importance in educational computing. Reliability implies that the computers, terminals and programs very seldom go wrong and can be repaired very quickly when they do. Resilience implies that the systems will tolerate mishandling without producing errors or unexpected results. Here again there are direct parallels with other pieces of equipment used in education and training, for example the overhead projector. So long as the equipment is used only peripherally, to support a relatively minor part of the teaching, then it can be abandoned if it goes wrong without serious inconvenience to the teacher or his students. However, as the use of the technique develops, it will come to play a more central role and the teacher will come to depend on its continued availability. Once CAL ceases to be a gimmick and is used seriously to provide learning opportunities which cannot easily be provided by other means, then it cannot be discarded lightly just because the computer is not available or the CAL program has gone wrong.

In the case of the computer and the terminals, reliability and resilience are familiar concepts, requiring that the electronic equipment should not go wrong, be easily repairable and should be student-proof. Computer programs are rather different. Unlike equipment with moving parts they cannot wear out and so, once they are free of errors and working correctly they will continue to do so for ever. The difficulty comes in ensuring that they do not contain any errors in the first place. Because the computer has no innate common sense, it must be given precise instructions on how to handle the input it is given. It is fatally easy to assume that the student using the CAL package will always input predictable messages and to ignore the probability that the unexpected will happen. Hence it is important that CAL programs are sufficiently resilient to cope with erroneous input without producing nonsensical output. Writing high quality CAL programs which are both reliable and resilient is a demanding task which should not be undertaken lightly. If a project intends to develop a number of programs it will probably be better to use a specialist programmer as part of the development team in the same way as a specialist photographer or graphics designer might be used in the production of other teaching media. Alas, for financial or other reasons, this is not always possible.

The Costs of Educational Computing

The costs of teaching with the aid of computers are comprised of two main components, the costs of designing and producing the CAL packages and the costs of providing and operating the equipment needed to deliver the packages. Traditionally, computer assisted learning has been regarded as an expensive educational aid. The reality is more complex, because the costs of CAL can vary considerably depending on the kind of CAL and the way in which the computing resources are organised and paid for. Further, they must be compared with the real costs of teaching by other means — also a very variable sum — and the comparison must recognise that CAL can be used for alternative or new kinds of teaching. The cost-effectiveness of CAL is therefore a complex issue. In this section we will examine briefly some of the factors which contribute to the costs.

The Costs of the Packages

The parallels between the production of CAL packages and the production of learning packages using other media were remarked in Chapter 3. The process of design, production, evaluation and modification is very necessary for the creation of good educational packages but is also time-consuming and therefore expensive. As a very rough rule of thumb, it may take a teacher ten hours to prepare each hour of a lecture course; the preparation of a package which will take a student about one hour to complete may involve between 50 and 200 hours' work. Computer assisted learning packages are no exception to this general rule and the resources needed to produce them should not be underestimated. The cost is largely independent of the number of students who will use the package and so it is attractive to consider increasing the potential audience by making the same packages available in a number of different institutions. This implies rather more generality than would normally be found in a learning package intended for use with a single, well defined group of students in one institution, and thus, a small but inevitable increase in costs. Care must be taken to make the subject material applicable to different students and also to write the CAL programs in a common dialect of the programming language — a sort of Queen's English — which is easily transferable to different computer systems.

The costs of delivering CAL materials to the students are more visible than the development costs. Again CAL is not unique in this respect, for other media such as tape slide and video also require special facilities for their use. Terminal based CAL needs a suitable computer, terminals, and some means of connecting the two, to be available at times that are convenient for the students. Systems which provide a batch service, for computer managed learning for example, can dispense with the terminals and communication facilities and so are inherently cheaper.

The Costs of Computers

Perhaps the cheapest way of obtaining the computer resources for teaching with computers is to use the surplus time on an existing computer system which provides a general computing service to the institution or was purchased for some other main application. There is usually some spare capacity available on such systems, and this surplus can be used for CAL without adding significantly to the overall computing costs. If the resources used are truly marginal then the real add-on costs of CAL will be very small. However, if the demand on resources grows then the computer centre may be forced to buy extra equipment or to employ more staff. Part or all of these costs will be directly attributable to the CAL activity, and this will then seem much more expensive. If the necessary facilities are provided by a computer system that is dedicated to educational computing, then all the costs can be said to be due to CAL and are very visible. This is the price that must be paid for the autonomy which comes from owning and operating your own computer.

The Costs of Terminals

Similar considerations apply to the provision of terminals and communications facilities. Where terminals are already provided as part of an institution-wide computing service, it may be possible to make use of them for CAL purposes. The additional cost will be minimal until such time as the demand imposed by CAL necessitates the purchase of additional terminals. At this point the costs again become visible.

In general, the more sophisticated the terminal the more expensive it is, and so terminal costs can be reduced by avoiding the use of complex graphics except where the presentation of the subject material warrants it. The cost per student can also be halved by designing some CAL packages so that they can be used by pairs of students working at a single terminal instead of providing each student with his own terminal. Finally, costs can be further minimised by making intelligent use of other media in the package. For example, where the aim of the CAL component is to enable the student to study the simulated behaviour of some geographical feature, it may be better — and cheaper — to provide all the background material for the experiment in printed form, rather than to use the CAL program as a page turner. If the length of time spent at the terminal is reduced, then not only may fewer terminals be needed but the costs of other computer resources will fall.

One of the problems of using spare capacity on an existing system is that the facilities may not always be available at convenient times for CAL work. The system will be scheduled to accommodate its major — and paying — users, and it is unfortunate if this means that the only time available at low cost is during the evening or very early morning, and is subject to interruption because of maintenance or other work. This conflicts with the idea of computer assisted learning as an open access resource enabling students to study as and when they want to. Computer assisted and computer managed learning applications which use a batch method of access are relatively immune from this problem because they can conveniently be scheduled in with other work. Since the user is not expecting an immediate response from the computer, some slack can be left in the system to allow for delays due to unexpected interruptions, such as breakdowns, and so the impact on the students can be minimised.

The cost of operating a terminal based CAL system is usually expressed in terms of the cost per student hour, that is the costs of one student studying CAL material at a terminal for one hour. Where batch methods are used then the key figure is the cost of running a single student's input through the CAL program. The costs for computer managed learning are more usually given as the cost for taking a student through one of the modules in the course, or the cost of managing a student through a complete course.

It is important to realise that the rather simplistic view of costs described above is complicated by the financial procedures operated by most educational and training organisations. Thus one set of costs are apparent to the teacher or instructor, another to his department and a third to the organisation as a whole. So while it may be sensible for the individual teacher to regard the costs of using an existing central computing service as minimal, the organisation may see a very different picture. After all, if a significant number of teachers started to make use of the facilities then it might be necessary to make some expensive additions to maintain the same level of service.

Cost-effectiveness

The costs visible to the teacher, his department and the organisation will vary depending on the level at which the computing facilities are purchased and operated. The cost part of the cost-effectiveness calculation must therefore take into account the situation as it affects CAL and compare it with the situation affecting other forms of teaching. For the comparison to be meaningful, the costs must be compared at each of the levels. If the teacher can replace or augment experimental equipment which comes out of his own departmental budget by CAL methods supported by a computer service paid for from central institution funds, then the CAL system will look very cheap and attractive. The central administration may of course hold the opposite view.

The other side of the cost-effectiveness calculation concerns the effectiveness of teaching and learning. Here too the problem is one of comparing unlike with unlike. Educational computing provides alternative means of achieving educational aims – and sometimes the means of achieving aims which cannot be reached by conventional methods. It is very difficult to make quantitative comparisons between different educational attainments and to place some monetary value on qualitative gains. In some situations the decision is quite clear cut because the choice is between using a particular piece of equipment of known cost, or replacing it with a CAL package, the cost of which can also be calculated. A student's time can also be quantified and costed, but his intuitive understanding of a subject can not. We must beware therefore of oversimplifying the cost-effectiveness justification for educational computing. With different presentations the figures can be made to look inviting or damning.

In training establishments, more attention is usually paid to the costs of using different teaching methods, so that the comparison is easier and more meaningful. Instructors are often aware of how much their activities are costing their department and the organisation, and there is an interest in reducing the costs of training whilst maintaining or improving the quality.

In real terms, the costs of CAL are usually rather higher than for using other media, comparable perhaps with that of individual or small group tuition, or of laboratory work at university level. Appropriately used, its effectiveness is considerable so that overall, educational computing could be said to provide better learning opportunities albeit at a higher cost. Because of the complexity of measuring the costs and educational effectiveness of educational computing and alternative methods, individual judgements as to whether CAL or CML should be used in a particular application must be based on the circumstances of that individual case.

7 MANAGING THE CAL INNOVATION

Education and training involve complex systems concerned with students, teachers and parents, resources such as schools and colleges and their equipment, administrators to manage the institutions, and society or industry as the ultimate benefactors of the system. Into this complex system of interrelated groups of protagonists, each with his own aims and objectives, we seek to introduce a change in the methods of teaching and learning, based on the use of the computer.

Pressures on the Innovation

Whatever the aims and objectives of the CAL development project, it requires a favourable environment since, if it is to be successful, it must operate within a variety of constraints and respond to a variety of pressures, both at a national and at a local level. Some of the more significant of these are shown in Figure 7.1. In particular, national and institutional politics, technological pressures – the resources available to education in general and to the institution in particular – and pressures from society or industry, influence the development of computer assisted and computer managed learning.

Political and Social Pressures

At a national level, the pressures vary from country to country. Different national educational systems present different educational needs, and different national perceptions of the roles and relative importance of education compared with other services have influenced the level, and the means, of funding computer assisted learning. The initial stimulus for educational innovation at a national level may come from within the education system itself or from outside it. The political response to this stimulus is often the provision of funding for research or development, on either a co-ordinated or *ad hoc* basis.

A frequent external stimulus has been the political awakening to a national need, perhaps worsening staff-student ratios or a widespread deficiency of some basic skill. The early development of CAL in North America, and later in Europe and the Soviet Union, was largely in response to such external pressures. A rapid increase in student numbers was not matched by an increase in the teaching staff and so there was a need for techniques which would enable teachers and

Figure 7.1: Interrelated Pressures on Education and Training

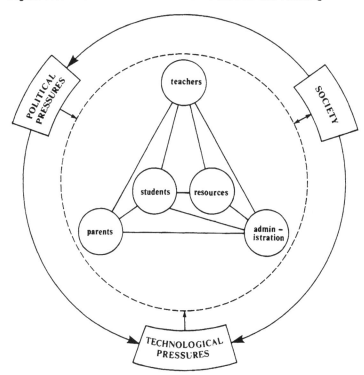

trainers to be more cost-effective. Computer assisted learning was seen to be a suitable educational prosthetic which would extend the power and range of the teacher, enabling him to handle more students without additional effort. More recently, similar arguments have been used in support of CAL in several developing countries. In practice as we have seen, CAL tends to improve the effectiveness of certain kinds of learning but, with a few exceptions, usually at additional cost. Nevertheless, the claim that CAL can save time and money is still advanced as one of the justifications for many projects, at a national, institutional and departmental level.

Even when a national need has been identified, the political response cannot be certain. It depends on the value that is placed on education compared with other areas of national spending, and on the way in which the educational system is organised. In general the need must be apparent to the funding agencies and thus a nationally perceived need is more likely to be answered by funding at a national level than by local funding from an individual institution. Where the education system is administered on a local level and the innovation is nationally funded, then problems may arise, particularly at the end of the project when the local authorities or institutions themselves are expected to assume the ongoing running costs.

Co-ordinated National Projects

In addition to initiatives from individual institutions, funded either from internal budgets or through one or more of the traditional funding agencies, a number of countries have organised co-ordinated national projects to develop and promote computer assisted learning.

One of the earliest of the European national programs was in West Germany where the government provided major support for the development of CAL between 1967 and 1975. The organisation was complicated by a division of responsibility; in Germany, education services are provided by the individual states while the responsibility for scientific research and development lies with the Federal government. Thus the development of CAL necessitated co-operation between the central government who were concerned with the technical and research aspects, and the local government who carried out the actual implementation in specially designated 'model' schools. The final decision as to whether CAL should be adopted in the schools was left with local government. Inevitably this divided responsibility led to some problems, particularly at the end of the funding period when the local government was asked to take the ongoing costs of individual developments on to its local budgets.

The French National Experiment in educational computing began in 1970 and was directed towards secondary education. Its goal was to develop, not only teaching with computers but also teaching about computers as discussed in Chapter 5. Like much of the French education system, it was highly centralised and controlled by the Ministry of Education. Its strategy was to provide intensive in-service courses in computing and CAL for a nucleus of teachers, to provide them with computing facilities in their schools, and then to use this nucleus of trained teachers to produce CAL materials and disseminate their ideas and expertise to their colleagues. Co-ordination for the ongoing use and further development of CAL continued under the aegis of the Ministry of Education.

The wide-scale development of CAL in the United Kingdom was first proposed in the late 1960s and was promoted by a quasi non-government organisation called the National Development Programme in Computer

Assisted Learning over the period 1973-1977. The National Programme funded projects in a wide range of subject areas, both in secondary and tertiary education, and in military and industrial training. It laid considerable emphasis on evaluation of the projects and on their plans for long-term survival. The Programme included formative and summative educational evaluation as well as a study of the financial and managerial performance of the projects. Some of the evaluation was carried out by the projects themselves and this was complemented by independent assessments from external evaluation agencies. The National Programme also stressed communication between CAL practitioners, organising a number of seminars and projects to promote the exchange of ideas, expertise and CAL packages.

Institutional Pressures

Local institutional politics defy generalisation but are perhaps the most potent forces acting on educational innovation; success at working within the specific institutional framework is one of the keys to the long-term viability of a CAL development project. Within the institution, politics are often bound up with societal pressures – the educational or training requirements of the society for which the institution is working. To this end, the introduction of computer assisted learning, like any other educational innovation, should be addressed to meeting real needs.

Technological Pressures

Finally, since most CAL projects, at least in their infancy and adolescence, use existing computing facilities, they must operate with what is available, rather than exploit the full potential of computer technology. Even when the resources are generous, the technology is a limiting factor because it has been developed for purposes other than education and training. For example, terminals designed specifically for CAL are rare because there is little money available for development and manufacturers perceive a relatively small market for such a specialist terminal.

CAL Development Projects

Most CAL projects fall into one of three functional groups:
- subject based projects,
- institutional projects,
- CAL exchange projects.

Subject Based Projects

First there are the projects that find their origins in a particular subject area or within a particular teaching department. The projects were first set up in response to a local need and are often staffed by the subject teachers who first realised the need for the innovation and who themselves benefit from it. As the projects mature, they tend to continue with their special interests, perhaps collaborating with similar specialists in other institutions, although some have diversified by accident or design into other subject areas. Organisationally, they are likely to be small and straightforward, primarily involving a few teaching staff with some educational and computing support, either from other departments in the institution (such as the educational development unit and the computer centre) or from specialist staff who are part of the project.

Institutional Projects

The second group is of projects that were set up to develop and support computer assisted learning within their institutions across a range of departments and subject areas. It includes some projects which, although originally limited to a single department or subject, grew to become interested in other areas and able to support CAL on a pan-institutional basis. Sometimes, teachers are reluctant to adopt new techniques that have been originated or are promoted by other departments in the institution, and so a project that has grown in this way may have problems of credibility. Alternative parents are the education development unit or the computer centre, either of which may have an interest in CAL as an interdisciplinary subject. Which of these origins is best for providing a credible, useful and secure base for CAL development depends entirely on the local politics of the institution and on the project staff. If it is to be useful in helping teachers to be aware of the possibilities and limitations of CAL, then the project must be able to provide information, training and support for both the educational and computing aspects. This implies the availability of educationalists and computer specialists to complement the activities of the subject teachers from user departments. Ultimately the security of the project — its long-term viability — should depend on its success, although the more cynical would say that it depends on its apparent success and political support. Its success is largely dependent on its credibility, for if potential users cannot be persuaded to sample its wares then it will never have the opportunity to prove whether it can be successful. Some institutions may give credibility to innovations established in other departments on the principle that success begets success; others will shun an evangelist from another department because of interdepartmental rivalries, yet welcome an independent educational consultant.

CAL Exchange Projects

The primary function of the third kind of project is to promote the inter-institutional exchange of CAL packages. We have already seen that the development of good packages requires substantial resources and that it is therefore desirable to use packages as widely as possible so as to spread the development costs over a large number of students. Moving a CAL package from one institution to another poses two problems; the transfer of the educational material to a new environment and the transfer of the CAL programs to a new computer system. Different CAL package exchange projects tackle these two aspects in different ways. Some concentrate on a single subject area and/or a restricted target audience, for example undergraduate level chemistry teaching, and so minimise the problems of transferring educational materials between disparate institutions. Others seek to edit the packages they receive to make them more generally applicable to a range of educational environments. This may require considerable resources to carry out the necessary adaptations. Similar strategies have been adopted to ease the problems of transferring the computer programs, with some projects specialising in one particular kind of computer while others impose rigid programming standards to minimise the changes needed to enable the programs to run on another machine.

Promoting Computer Assisted Learning

Teachers and trainers first get involved in computer assisted learning for a variety of reasons; some because they believe that the technique will save them time and effort, others because of the intellectual challenge that it provides, and others because of the lure of the computer. Now, CAL is a difficult subject to evangelise in writing. Its great strengths are in the different kinds of learning opportunities that it can provide, kinds of learning which are impractical in other media and so cannot be demonstrated in the pages of a book or the words of a learned paper. The most effective means of discussing CAL is through the use of real CAL packages that demonstrate the different techniques available. If these are to be credible, then they must be written to address real teaching problems, preferably problems that are familiar to the teacher trying out the package, rather than to illustrate individual points or facilities. Again we should remember that the CAL program is likely to be only one component of a complete teaching package. If so, then it must be seen by the teacher in this context. A departmentally based project is likely to have fewer difficulties in providing good demonstration packages in one or two subject areas, than a project which aims to promote CAL across the institution and which therefore needs packages in a wide range of subjects.

The First Steps

A first essay into using CAL is perhaps best achieved by using existing materials imported from elsewhere and adapted if necessary — not by designing and producing new packages from scratch. This reduces the resources needed to get started and allows the teachers to concentrate on the use rather than on the production of CAL materials. Here again, a broadly based project must be in a position to provide information on, and to acquire, a wide range of suitable packages, and then to make them available in its own institution. The project may need to help in transferring the CAL programs on to a new computer system and must support the teachers in developing or modifying the packages to meet local needs. Different teachers in different institutions will teach the same subject in different ways and will want the CAL package to reflect their own preferences. Only rarely will a package, developed at one institution, be completely acceptable to teachers in another; local adaptation should be expected and welcomed, not avoided. As the package is used by successive groups of students and the teachers become more familiar with the techniques, the adaptations can lead to the development of new materials designed specifically to meet the teacher's needs.

Encouraging CAL Authors

One of the less frequently admitted motives for participating in the development of CAL is the kudos which attaches to those involved. Alas, in the university environment, kudos and advancement are generally acquired by research work and publications, rather than by good teaching or developing new teaching materials. This poses a problem for the production of new CAL packages, that of motivating and encouraging the author. Educational research based on CAL can, directly or indirectly, help a university teacher's career, but the production of teaching packages, which may take several weeks of effort for each hour of material written and evaluated, does not. Clearly some means of reward is needed to encourage the development of good teaching materials, whether or not they are based on CAL or some other media. A number of solutions have been proposed. One suggestion is that users of CAL materials should pay a royalty to the package author or authors, each time a student works through a package. This would be equivalent to the system whereby an author receives a royalty on each copy of his book, but with a recording mechanism built into the CAL package to keep accounts of the number of times it is used and the consequent payments to be made. Perhaps a simpler, more fundamental solution would be for universities to acknowledge that since they are involved in teaching as well as research, they should give credit for teaching work too. Fortunately, the problem is usually serious only in universities; in other educational institutions and training, the focus is already on teaching and instruction and so the anomaly does not arise.

Computer Managed Learning

The introduction of computer managed learning requires a rather different kind of support. Because of the relatively large resources necessary to produce good CML systems, an institution is more likely to import an existing, proven system than develop its own, and because of the size of the systems they present greater problems in transferring them on to a new computer. Unlike most CAL applications, CML does not always depend on the immediate availability of the computer and can therefore be used very effectively by batch computing methods instead of requiring terminals. This means that teachers can use CML to support their teaching and their students' learning even if they do not have a computer or a terminal in their classroom – or even in their institution. Thus the computing start up costs for CML can be very low.

In contrast to CAL where pilot usage may only involve a small part of a course, CML requires a substantial educational commitment if it is to be effective, with relatively large parts of the course supported by the system. Despite this initial hurdle, CML can be introduced gradually, by first using it to support existing course structures, and only developing new courses to take advantage of the extended facilities, when the teachers are familiar with its more limited use. From time to time, with or without the support of CML, courses are changed to reflect evolving educational aims or syllabus changes, and at these times the computer can be introduced as an aid to course management, enabling different kinds of courses to be provided, without incurring large overheads in course redevelopment. In this way the introduction of CML is perceived as an aid to the teacher and trainer rather than as an unwelcome intrusion that forces them to spend time and effort altering existing courses.

The use of CML also affects educational and training administrators as well as teachers. The introduction of computer assisted learning as a tutorial or simulation tool impacts on the classroom teacher and his students; computer management of learning provides more complete and timely information for the students, teachers, course directors, administrators and planners. The role of the project team is thus extended to provide support for other staff who would not normally be directly involved in educational development, and who have different motivations and perceptions of their institution from the teaching staff.

A Model for Managing Innovation

It is a fact of life that the management of educational innovation plays an important role in determining whether new methods or techniques are accepted or discarded. The success of educational computing in a particular institution depends on many factors. Some of these, for example the use of CAL or CML to meet real teaching or learning needs, are educational, while others, such as the ability of the developer to work within the political framework of the institution, are managerial. As with many other educational technologies, the introduction and development of educational computing requires resources of people and facilities. These resources are usually limited within the institution and available only at the expense of some other activity, and this adds necessity to the desirability of using the resources to the best effect. This section outlines one way in which the innovation may be encouraged and managed by a project set up to provide CAL support for an educational or training institution.

First, the project should provide a wide range of information on the milieu of educational computing such as general descriptions of CAL and CML, descriptions of specific educational computing projects, the implications of educational computing for curriculum design and assessment, and the technology associated with CAL and CML. This can be made available through a variety of media, possibly using the computer to index the material or to facilitate serendipitous browsing as discussed in Chapter 2, and supported by seminar demonstrations and personal discussions.

Development Proposals

Teachers who are interested in the possibility of using the computer to support their teaching should then be encouraged to discuss their ideas with the project staff. If appropriate, then these discussions will culminate in a written proposal setting out the aspirations and intended course of the development. The proposal should consider:

   − the educational environment, the course and the students,
   − the particular problems which the development seeks to solve,
   − the alternative solutions considered,
   − a description of the proposed development,

- the resource implications for the development and the subsequent use of the new teaching materials,
- the management of the development,
- how the work is to be evaluated to assess its cost, achievements and success.

All these are standard points which should be considered for any educational development and the initial planning which is forced by such a document is most useful in clarifying thoughts and objectives at an early stage.

Critical Examination

The development proposal, and in particular its resource implications, should be examined by a steering committee comprised of teachers and administrators, including those who control the resources that the development proposes to use. This step enables the institution to appreciate its commitment to the development, the resources it will need and the benefits it should bring. Since the resources available in the institution are likely to be limited, the committee should seek to allocate them to the greatest effect, hence it should be looking for developments which make the best and appropriate use of the technology and show good potential for long-term educational benefit to justify the resources consumed.

The steering committee should continue to monitor the progress of development projects and their final evaluation. This is not intended to supplant the internal management of the project which should be responsible for its daily running. The organisation of the internal management should, of course, vary for each individual development, taking into consideration its size, resource requirements, personal preferences and style.

Just as educational computing or any other kind of educational technology is not a universal panacea for educational problems, so there is no magic formula for assuring the success of educational computing. However, appropriately used, to meet real needs, it can be used effectively as one of the tools to support — not to replace — teachers and trainers.

BIBLIOGRAPHY

There is an abundance of literature on educational computing in the form of short papers describing specific research and development projects, and on some of the theoretical aspects and implications. The problem in compiling a bibliography is therefore, not to accumulate sufficient references, but to restrict it to those which are relevant. This bibliography has been limited to a few key books, reports and papers, selected because they amplify various topics in the text and/or indicate further directions for study.

1. Computers in Education and Training

Carnegie Commission on Higher Education. *The Fourth Revolution; Instructional Technology in Higher Education* (McGraw Hill, New York, 1972). This book examines the impact of many aspects of new technologies, particularly in instruction and libraries, on administrators, teachers and students.

Levien, R. E. et al. *The Emerging Technology; Instructional Uses of the Computer in Higher Education* (McGraw Hill, New York, 1972). The companion volume, *The Fourth Revolution* examines the impact of technology on higher education; this book concentrates on the current and future use of the computer for research, administration and instruction.

Oettinger, A. G., with Marks, S. *Run Computer Run; the Mythology of Educational Innovation* (Harvard Studies in Technology and Society, Harvard University Press, Cambridge, Massachusetts, 1969). As the use of CAL spread in the late 1960s, there was considerable optimism about its rapid impact on education. This book strikes a warning note and seeks to temper the euphoria with a measure of scepticism.

2. Computer Assisted Learning

Ellis, A. B. *The Use and Misuse of Computers in Education* (McGraw Hill, New York, 1974). Written in a North American context, this book considers some of the implications of computing for education and describes in detail the development of two large scale projects, NEEDS (A system for secondary school administration) and ISVD (Information System for Vocational Decisions).

Hooper, R., and Toye, I. *Computer Assisted Learning in the United Kingdom. Some Case Studies* (Council for Educational Technology, London, 1975). The book brings together eighteen case studies of CAL and CML applications in secondary and higher education, and training, and includes a chapter on artificial intelligence in education.

Kemmis, S., Atkin, R., and Wright, E. *How Do Students Learn? — Working Papers on Computer Assisted Learning*, Occasional paper no. 5 (Centre for Applied Research in Education, University of East Anglia, 1977). This lengthy report contains nine theoretical papers on the evaluation of student learning, understanding CAL and learning theory. It includes a number of educational profiles of CAL projects in the United Kingdom.

Lecarme, O., and Lewis, R. (eds.). *Computers in Education* (North Holland, Amsterdam, 1975). These are the proceedings, in two volumes, of an international conference held in Marseille in 1975, containing a large number of papers in French and English, that describe CAL and CML projects in Europe, North America and elsewhere.

3. Using Computer Assisted Learning

Dyer, C. A. *Preparing for Computer Assisted Learning* (Educational Technology Publications, Englewood Cliffs, New Jersey, 1972). Although this book involves the reader with too many of the detailed computing aspects of CAL, such as writing programs for a specific type of computer, the middle section contains some useful material on the production of tutorial style CAL packages (see page 47).

McDonald, B., Atkin, R., Jenkins, D., and Kemmis, S. 'The Educational Evaluation of NDPCAL', *British Journal of Educational Technology*, vol. 8, no. 3 (1977). This paper describes the aims and techniques, and summarises the conclusions of the independent evaluation of the projects sponsored by the United Kingdom National Development Programme in Computer Assisted Learning (see page 50).

4. Computer Managed Learning

Anderson, R. C., Kulhavey, R. W., and Andre, T. 'Feedback Procedures in Programmed Instruction', *Journal of Educational Psychology*, vol. 62 (1971), pp. 148-56. It is usually assumed that if feedback is to be effective then it must be given to the student immediately or very rapidly. As this paper shows, the situation is more complex than this and in some situations (see for example page 61) the learning may be improved if the feedback is delayed.

Baath, J. A., and Mansson, N. O. *CADE — A System for Computer Assisted Distance Education* (Hermods Skola, Malmo, Sweden, 1977). CADE, an advanced CML system developed in Sweden to support distance education, has a very different philosophy from many earlier CML systems. This report describes its development and use.

Byrne, C. J. *Computerised Question Banking Systems* (National Development Programme in Computer Assisted Learning, London 1975). This provides a good introduction to the rationale and practice of item banking discussed on page 64, with descriptions of some item banking projects. It includes a comprehensive bibliography.

Crocker, A. C. *Statistics for the Teacher* (National Foundation for Education Research, Slough, 1974). This introduction to test and item analysis does not lead the reader into deep mathematical waters and is to be recommended to those who wish to understand the basic methods discussed briefly in Chapter 4. A full treatment of the subject is given by Guilford (q.v.).

Guilford, J. P. *Fundamental Statistics in Psychology and Education* (McGraw Hill, Kogakusha, 1973). This is a standard work of reference for those engaged in the statistical analysis of tests and examinations referred to in Chapter 4. A brief introduction to the subject is provided by Crocker (q.v.).

LAMSAC. *Towards a Computer Based Education Management Information System* (Local Authorities Management Services and Computer Committee, London, 1974). The report discusses the need for a computer based information system for secondary education and suggests how this might be implemented (see page 70).

McMahon, H. F. 'Progress and Prospects in Computer-Managed Learning in the United Kingdom', *Programmed Learning and Educational Technology*, vol. 15, no. 2 (1978), pp. 104-13. This paper is a résumé of the state of the art of CML in the United Kingdom at the end of 1977. It includes brief descriptions of all the major systems extant at that time and discusses their potential for the future.

Murray, D. 'Rasch Item Analysis and Scaling', *Proceedings of the British Psychological Society Annual Conference* (1975). This paper explains some of the mysteries of the Rasch method for context independent item analysis described briefly on page 66.

Skurnik, L. S., and Nuttal, D. L. 'Describing the Reliability of Examination', *The Statistician*, vol. 18, no. 2, pp. 119-29. This paper discusses the underlying principles of the Skurnik-Nuttal Measuremeter referred to on page 63, and how it may be used to relate the reliability of tests and examinations to the candidates' subsequent grades.

5. Informatics and Education

Lafond, C. 'Introducing Informatics and Using Computers in Teaching', in Jones, A., and Weinstock, H. (eds.), *Computer Based Science Instruction* (Centre Imago and the International Project UCODI, Louvain-La-Neuve, Belgium, 1977). The French National Experiment in CAL has applied informatics to the teaching-learning process (see page 82). This paper describes a number of CAL programs in use in French secondary education which follow this philosophy.

Makkar, L. 'Who needs Educating? Laymen or Computermen?', *Computer Bulletin* (London, June 1975), pp. 24-6. In this paper, Makkar summarises and justifies the case for computer awareness described on page 78, contrasting it with the traditional, technology-oriented approach of computer appreciation.

6. Technological Aspects

Cook, V. *The Human Factors Aspect of the Student/Terminal Interface in CAL Systems* (National Development Programme in Computer Assisted Learning, London, 1974). This report covers a multitude of factors to be considered when designing or using a CAL terminal. It includes a bibliography on the ergonomics of computer terminals (see page 88).

Fielden, J., and Pearson, P. K. *The Cost of Learning with Computers* (Council for Educational Technology, London, 1978). The educational computing projects sponsored by the United Kingdom National Development Programme in Computer Assisted Learning, were subject to detailed financial scrutiny. This is the final report of that evaluation, and expands on some of the points made on page 93.

Hunt, R., and Shelley, J. *Computers and Commonsense* (Prentice Hall International, London, 1975). Recommended reading for those who wish to plumb the mysteries of the computer's inner workings.

Leiblum, M. D. *An Analytical and Comparative Study of Computer-Assisted Instruction Programming Languages, Their Characteristics and Usage* (Katholieke Universiteit, Nijmegen, Netherlands, 1974). This is a comprehensive treatment of the CAL author languages referred to on page 91. It includes descriptions of some of the more common languages and a bibliography.

Pearson, P. K. *Costs of Education in the United Kingdom* (Council for Educational Technology, London, 1977). Before looking at the cost-effectiveness of CAL, we must be aware of the costs of teaching by other methods. This book provides a readable account of a methodology which can be used to assess the costs of education and some conclusions on the costs of teaching in 1977 (see page 93).

Zinn, D. *A Comparative Study of Languages for Programming Interactive Use of Computers in Instruction* (University of Michigan, Ann Arbor, 1969). Although dated, this is probably the most authoritative study of CAL author languages. It is certainly the most quoted (see page 91).

7. Managing the CAL Innovation

Darby, C. A., Korotkin, A. L., and Romashko, A. *The Computer in Secondary Schools; A Survey of its Instructional and Administrative Use* (Praeger Publishers, New York, 1972). This is the report of a detailed survey carried out in 1970, on the ways in which computers were used in secondary education in the United States of America. Although now dated, the summarised results and conclusions make interesting reading.

Hallworth, H. J., Brahan, J. W., Hart, J., Hunka, S., Lee, W., and Olivier, W. P. *Computer Aided Learning in the Federal Republic of Germany* (National Research Council of Canada, NRC 14946, 1974). This is an account of the way in which the CAL developments in West Germany were promoted. A number of the projects are described.

House, E. R. *The Politics of Educational Innovation* (McCutchan Publishing Corporation, California, 1974). Mandatory reading for all those entrepreneurs who seek to innovate, or administrators who seek to survive innovation. Written from an American experience of CAL, the parallels with other national environments are obvious.

Leiblum, M. D. 'A Pragmatic Approach to Initiating a Computer Assisted Instruction Service and some of the Problems Involved', in Hills, P. J., and Gilbert, K. (eds.), *Aspects of Educational Technology* XI (Kogan Page, London, 1977), pp. 448-53. In this paper, Leiblum describes the organisation and operation of the CAI project at the University of Nijmegen (see page 106).

GLOSSARY

This glossary contains definitions of many of the key terms found in educational computing. It does not aspire to be a comprehensive glossary on computers and computing but does include some terms which, although not central to this text, occur in general computing parlance and may be encountered by the CAL practitioner.

Alphameric Terminal. A terminal (q.v.) which can handle responses and display messages composed of letters, digits and a number of special symbols, but cannot display complex diagrams or pictures.

Artificial Intelligence. Quasi-intelligent behaviour exhibited by artificially created systems. The term is used to describe systems which can emulate human thinking processes, such as conversation in natural language, quite closely although not exactly.

Authentic Labour. Something the student must do as an integral part of his learning and which makes a valuable contribution to it.

Author. Someone who writes learning packages — in this context, CAL packages.

Author Language. A programming language (q.v.) designed specifically for the task of writing CAL programs.

Batch Computing. In batch computing, the user prepares his input away from the computer and then submits it to a queue of jobs waiting to be run. After it has been processed by the computer, the resulting output is returned to the user. There is a delay inherent in batch computing due to the necessity of moving information from the user to the computer and back again.

CAL Package. A learning package, comprising a number of different contributions to a specific topic, using a variety of media including CAL, in an appropriate combination.

CAL Program. A computer program (q.v.) which provides a particular learning opportunity for its user.

Calculator Use of CAL. A form of CAL in which the student uses the computer as a sophisticated calculator to reduce the arithmetic burden of learning.

Computer. A machine for storing and manipulating data. The way in which it moves data about and combines or compares small pieces of data inside itself, is controlled by a set of instructions called a program. Different programs will instruct the computer to work in different ways, to process different kinds of data for different purposes.

Computer Aided Instruction and *Computer Assisted Instruction* – *CAI*. Teaching with the aid of a computer. One of a number of near synonyms for computer assisted learning but with different connotations in Europe (where it can imply tutorial CAL) and in North America (where it is used as a general description).

Computer Assisted Learning – *CAL*. Teaching with the aid of a computer. This is the term most commonly used in the United Kingdom.

Computer Based Education – *CBE* and *Computer Based Learning* – *CBL*. Two more synonyms for teaching with the aid of a computer.

Computer Managed Instruction – *CMI* and *Computer Managed Learning* – *CML*. The use of the computer to assist the teacher, instructor and administrator with the routine management tasks in teaching and learning, such as assessment, guidance, record keeping and reporting.

Conjectural CAL. The use of the computer to assist the student in his manipulation and testing of ideas and hypotheses. It is based on the concept that knowledge can be created through the student's experiences; its emphasis is on the student's exploration of information on a particular topic.

Conversational Computing. In conversational or interactive computing, the user communicates with the computer through a terminal (q.v.) and obtains a very rapid response from the computer, typically within a second, to the messages he sends. Because of the immediacy of the dialogue between the user and the computer, it can be thought of as a conversation.

Courseware. The teaching materials used in educational computing. It may be contrasted with hardware (the physical computer) and software (the programs that make the computer operate).

Criterion-referenced Testing. In testing for diagnostic purposes, and particularly in training, the aim is to ascertain whether the student has mastered a particular objective or set of objectives. The test therefore refers to a given criterion.

Data. Any numbers, words, or other collections of facts that are flowing about a system, particularly into, out of, or around a computer. The word is often used loosely and confused with information; information is useful — data is not necessarily so but may yield information. Data is a collective noun but is used for both singular and plural purposes and is usually given a singular verb.

Data Base. An organised and structured collection of data (q.v.), such as a set of student records, which can be searched to yield useful information.

Dedicated. An adjective applied to a resource, usually in this context a computer, which is reserved for one special purpose and can therefore be organised in the best way for that one purpose.

Dialogue. The sequence of messages between the user and the computer.

Discrimination Index. The indication of a question's ability to distinguish between good and bad students. A question, or item, which is answered correctly by the best students and incorrectly by the worst, will have a discrimination index of 1 or near to 1, while a question which all students irrespective of ability get right or wrong, will have a discrimination index which is very low.

Distance Learning. A teaching/learning environment in which the student is physically distant from his tutor and the central institution, for example, a correspondence course.

Documentation. The narrative description, notes and diagrams which help to explain the workings of a computer program (q.v.) for someone who is unfamiliar with it. It might also contain flow-charts, operating instructions, a set of test data, sample output, and teacher and student notes, though it is unlikely that each reader would need all of these items.

Drill and Practice. A learning technique in which the student is presented with a structured succession of exercise questions designed to give him practice in a particular subject area. The sequence of examples can be arranged so as to provide questions of a certain difficulty, or graded in severity to probe the student's learning difficulties, and may be interspersed with teaching materials to provide remediation in areas of weakness.

Educational Computing. The use of the computer in the teaching/learning process; teaching with the aid of computers as opposed to teaching about computers.

Emancipatory CAL. The use of the computer as a means of reducing the student's workload, for example as an aid for numerical calculations or for information retrieval.

Facility Value. A measure of how easy or how hard a question is. A question which is answered correctly by most students, an easy question, will have a very high facility value while one which most students get wrong will have a very low value.

Frame. A single step in a tutorial CAL sequence, usually consisting of some narrative followed by a question, the processing of the student's response, and finally the actions to be taken following each possible type of response.

Graphics Terminal. A terminal (q.v.) which, in addition to displaying messages composed of letters, digits and symbols, can also display line drawings, graphs and maps. Some can also be used with special sets of characters such as Russian and Arabic.

Hardware. The actual machinery, made of metal, glass and plastic, of the computing system. It may be contrasted with the software (the programs) and the courseware (the teaching materials) of educational computing.

Inauthentic Labour. Something the student must do as an accessory to his learning, but is not an integral part of the learning and is not valued for its own sake.

Informatics. The study of information, the way we manipulate and use it, and its impact on society.

Information. Meaningful numbers, words, or other collections of facts input to, output from, or flowing around a system. The word is often used loosely and confused with data. The two are not synonymous; information is useful – data is not necessarily so, but may yield information. Information in one sense implies surprise – something which was not known before.

Information Retrieval. The searching of a large quantity of data – perhaps a data base (q.v.) – to elicit useful information.

Instructional CAL. A form of CAL akin to programmed learning in which the student is led through the learning material via a structured question and answer dialogue. The focus of the instruction is on the subject material and on the student's mastery of the various concepts within it.

Interactive Computing. In interactive or conversational computing, the user communicates with the computer through a terminal (q.v.) and obtains a very rapid response from the computer, typically within a second, to the messages he sends. This gives an immediacy to the interaction between the user and the computer which is not possible in batch computing.

Item Analysis. A statistical evaluation of the performance of individual questions or items, in a test. Two of the common measures calculated are the item's facility value (how easy or difficult the question is) and the discrimination index (how well it distinguishes between good and bad students).

Item Bank. A collection of test questions, together with their characteristics — facility values and discrimination indices, dates and conditions of previous use — which may be used for constructing new tests. The collection may be held on index cards or in a computer system to facilitate the automatic construction of tests.

Keyword Matching. The identification of key words within the student's response that correspond to entries in a list prespecified by the author, and subsequent matching of the given combination of these key words against the expected pattern.

Learning Package. A collection of one or more different contributions to a specific topic, using a variety of media in an appropriate combination, designed to help a student learn about the topic.

Model. An analogue of a real-life situation or system which can be studied to provide information about the probable behaviour of the real system. This enables the student to study systems which would otherwise be too expensive, too time-consuming or too dangerous. In a CAL context there is a distinction between simulation and modelling. A student using a CAL simulation may be encouraged to change its external conditions, but is prevented from altering the equations which govern its behaviour; in modelling, the student can be asked to specify some parts of the model or to construct it in its entirety.

Multiple Choice Question — MCQ. A question which is presented to the student with a number of alternative answers. The student must answer by selecting and indicating the answer or answers he believes are correct.

Norm-referenced Testing. The aim of a norm-referenced test is to grade the students tested, and to compare their performance with their peers and against a norm. This leads to tests in which the scores have a bell-shaped or normal distribution and a wide spread or deviation, so that they can be used to distinguish between individual students or set them into different grades.

On-Line. A terminal (q.v.) is said to be on-line when it is connected to the interactive computer system and ready for use. When it is disconnected then it is said to be off-line. The term on-line computing is sometimes used to mean interactive or conversation computing (q.v.).

Optical Mark Reader. A machine, connected to a terminal or computer system, that can sense the presence or absence of black marks in predetermined places on a sheet of paper or card. It provides a convenient means of entering survey data or test results into a computer system. The marks, usually short lines within marked areas on the paper, can be made with a fibre tip pen or medium pencil.

Printing Terminal. A terminal (q.v.) which displays the user's input and the output from the computer in a printed form on paper, rather than ephemerally on a screen. The user (the student) can then keep a permanent record of the dialogue for future reference.

Program. The set of instructions given to the computer to control the way in which it manipulates data.

Programming Languages. The set of instructions (the program) which controls the way in which the computer manipulates data for a particular problem, must specify in great detail what the computer is to do. The instruction must also be input to the computer in an intelligible form. Programming languages are used to bridge the communications gap between the author and the computer, allowing him to express his instructions in a convenient form, and supplying various checks to reduce the possibility of errors.

Rasch Method. The Rasch method provides a means of evaluating the performance of a test question (or item) that is independent of the exact way in which the question was used. Other statistics, such as the facility value and discrimination index, must be related to the group of students who answered the question and the other questions in the test.

Resource Management. The use of the computer to assist the teacher and administrator with the scheduling and inventory of resources used in the teaching or training process. It includes such applications as time-tabling and stock control.

Response. The response in interactive computing and CAL is usually taken to be the user's or student's input to the computer system, such as a request for information or the answer to a question. Since the computer is, or should be, the servant and not the master in this partnership, then it would be more appropriate to deem the computer's output to be the response.

Response Time. The response time of an interactive computer system is the average time that the user must wait for a reply to his input message. Typically this wait is under a second; if it rises appreciably above this then the delay becomes obtrusive and conversational computing becomes stilted.

Revelatory CAL. A form of CAL in which the user is guided through a process of discovery so that the subject matter and the underlying theory are progressively revealed to him as he proceeds through the CAL package. The computer acts as a mediator between the student and a hidden model of some real-life situation.

Routing. Guiding students through structured course materials based on the assumption that the majority of students should follow one of a limited number of well trodden paths.

Serendipity Learning. Learning by discovery as a result of browsing through a large collection of information, stored either in a library, a learning resource centre, or a computer system.

Short Answer Question. A question which requires a response in the form of a brief, constructed answer, perhaps a single sentence, rather than a selection from a number of alternative possible answers or the composition of an essay.

Simulation. An analogue of a real-life situation or system which can be studied to provide information about the real system. This enables the student to study systems which would otherwise be too expensive, too time-consuming or too dangerous. In a CAL context, there is a distinction between simulation and modelling. A student using a CAL simulation may be encouraged to change its external conditions but is prevented from altering the equations which govern its behaviour; in modelling, the student can be asked to specify some parts of the model or to construct it in its entirety.

Skurnik-Nuttal Measuremeter. The Measuremeter provides a practical indication of the usefulness of a norm-referenced test. It indicates the number of grades into which the students could be divided on the basis of the test, with a probability of 0.95 that each student be given the correct grade, the one above it or the one below.

Software. A collective noun for the programs used in a computing system. It may be contrasted with the hardware (the physical computer) and the courseware (the teaching materials) of educational computing.

Student Records. Collections of information about individual students and groups of students, including such things as: the courses they are studying, the history of their studies, their results in diagnostic tests and examinations, background information about their learning preferences, aspirations and problems, comments made about them by their teachers, home address, date of birth, and so on.

System. A set of components which, together, perform some function. The components are not necessarily electronic or mechanical; people and institutions, living organisms, chemical substances and atomic particles can all be part of systems. For example, a computer assisted learning system consists of computer hardware (the physical machinery), software (the programs), courseware (the learning packages), operators, authors, teachers and students. It is also in itself a part of a larger teaching system.

Teletype. The term is an abbreviation for teletypewriter and is used to describe a mechanical printing terminal that resembles a rather noisy electric typewriter or telex machine. It can only handle responses and display messages composed of letters, digits and a number of special symbols and displays the dialogue in a printed form on paper.

Terminal. A piece of equipment, connected to a computer, that incorporates some means for the user to send messages to the computer and for the computer to reply. Usually the user operates a typewriter-like keyboard for his input to the computer although some terminals have other, or additional, facilities. The computer output may be displayed on a television-like screen or printed on paper. (See also alphameric terminal, graphics terminal, teletype, printing terminal, visual display unit).

Test Analysis. A statistical evaluation of the performance of a test, based on the candidates' scores. It may also include analyses of the individual questions or items. The analysis may show the distribution of the scores, various statistical measures such as the mean, standard deviation and skew, the internal consistency of the test, and the Skurnik-Nuttal Measuremeter.

Timesharing. An alternative term for interactive computing, where the user communicates with the computer through a terminal (q.v.) and obtains a very rapid response from the computer. The speed of the computer enables it to do small pieces of work for each of several users in turn, so quickly that each is unaware that other people are using the machine simultaneously. This is analogous to the way in which cine pictures, shown in rapid succession, give the illusion of continuous motion.

Tutorial CAL. A synonym for instructional CAL, a form of CAL akin to programmed learning in which the student is led through the learning material via a structured question and answer dialogue. The focus of the instruction is on the subject material and on the student's mastery of the various concepts within it.

Visual Display Unit — VDU. A terminal which displays the user's input and the output from the computer on a television-like screen. Although VDUs have the disadvantage that no permanent record of the dialogue is made, they are generally much quieter than printing terminals and cheaper to run because they do not consume large quantities of paper.

INDEX

alphameric terminal 44
analysis: of items 63-4; of tests 61-3
applications of computers: education 13-14; industry and business 12, 75; research 12; society 80; teaching computing 12
artificial intelligence 33, 35
assessment 14, 55-60
authentic labour 33
awareness of computers 77-9

batch computing 45, 89-91; costs 95-6
behaviourist model of learning 22pp
biology application 29
books and other print media 38
browsing 34-5
business studies application 45

calculator use of CAL 31
careers counselling 72-3
commercial applications of computers 12
communications 87-8
computer: costs 85; description 79, 85; different kinds 86-7; operating costs 86, 90, 94; program 79-80; reliability 92-3; timesharing 86
computer aided instruction 14, 17
computer assisted instruction 17
computer assisted learning: costs 93-7, 99, 107; definition 15, 17; dialogue 23, 26, 31, 45; different types 22, calculator 31, conjectural 31-3, 82, drill and practice 27, emancipatory 33-6, instructional 22, revelatory 27-30, 82, tutorial 22; evaluation 50-1; justifications 18-19, 36; kinds of project 101-3, institution based 102, package exchange 103, subject based 101; package 37-43; program 37; project management 106; promotion 103-6; strengths and weaknesses 40
computer based education 18
computer based learning 18

computer managed learning 15, 17; assessment 53; careers counselling 72-3; computing considerations 87, 105; cycle 54-5; educational development support 105; library circulation 71-2; privacy 69-70; rationale 52; record keeping 69, 72; reporting 70-1; resource management 74; routing 68-9
conjectural CAL 31-3, 82
costs 93-7; budgets 96; CAL 93, 96, 99, 107; computers 85-93; cost-effectiveness 96; operating computers 86, 90, 94; other media 94; terminals 88-9, 95
criterion-referenced testing 14, 62, 63

demonstrations 103, 106
development 106-7
dialogue 23, 26, 31, 45
discrimination index 63
distance learning 73
documentation 49
drill and practice 27

education: aims 13; assessment 14; distance 73; locus of control of learning 14
education system: description 13; 98; in a CML environment 73; pressures on system 98
educational computing 18
educational development: CAL as part of 20; support for CML 105
electronics application 32
emancipatory CAL 33-6
errors in computer programs 79, 93
essay questions 56, 59
European CAL 19, 22, 98; France 100; United Kingdom 100-1; West Germany 100
evaluation: CAL packages 50-1; existing teaching methods 20; for costing 97

facility value 63
feedback 60-1

film media 38, 44
frame 23
France, National Experiment in CAL 100
funding for CAL 98

graphics terminal 44, 89
guidance: careers 72; through course material 68

histogram of test results 61
history application 33
hypothesis forming and testing 31

inauthentic labour 33
informatics: and CAL 82-4; definition 78
information retrieval 34
instructional CAL 22-7
instructors 39-40; motivation 104
interactive computing: computing demands 86; contrasted with batch 45, 90; costs 96
item: analysis 63; banking 64; discrimination index 63; facility value 63

justifications: for CAL 18, 36; for CML 52

keyboard skills 44
keyword matching 26

languages: for CAL 91-2; general purpose 91-2
learning environment 15; distance learning 73; flow of information 15; solitary or group learning 45
learning material: design and production 41, 47-50, 84; multimedia package 40; structure 22, 25, 26, 47, 68; transfer and adaptation 104
library circulation systems 71-2
locus of control of learning 14

mathematics application 32
medical application 29
models 28, 29, 30, 31; in electronics 32; in history 33; in mathematics 32
moderation of examination results 62
motivating CAL authors 104
multiple choice questions: in CAL 25; in CML 56-7

norm-referenced testing 62
North America, CAL 19, 22, 98
nuclear engineering application 28

optical mark reading 58

packages: design and production 41-5, 47-50, 84; multimedia 40; structure 22, 25, 26, 47, 68; transfer and adaptation 94, 104
Peter Principle 52
privacy 69-70
problem solving 81-2
program 79-80
programmed learning 19, 22
programming: CAL languages 91; errors 79, 93; for authors 49; for CAL 31; for non-specialists 77; for specialists 12; general purpose languages 91; reliability 93; teaching 12; transferability 94, 104
project management 106
project types: institution based 102; package exchange 103; subject based 101-2
promotion of CAL 103-4

Rasch Method 66
record keeping: in CAL programs 50; in CML systems 69, 72; privacy 69-70
reliability 92-3
research use of computers 12
resources management 71, 74-5
responses 23; keyword matching 26; matching 26; misspellings 27; multiple choice 25
revelatory CAL 27, 82
routing in CML systems 68-9
royalties 104

serendipity learning 34-6, 106
short answer questions 56, 59
simulation 28-30; business studies 45; display of output 44; genetics 29; medical education 29; nuclear engineering 28; statistics 28-9
Skinner's theory of conditioning 22
Skurnick-Nuttal Measuremeter 63
Soviet Union 19, 22, 98
staff-student ratios 19
statistics application 28
student records: description 17; in

CML systems 69, 72; privacy
69-70

tape slide 38
teachers 39-40; motivation 104-5
terminal: alphameric terminal 41,
88, 89; CAL 44, 89, 101; communications 87-8; costs 89,
95-6; description 41, 88-9
graphics 44, 89; reliability 93-4
testing: criterion-referenced 14, 62
discrimination index 63; essay
questions 56, 59; facility value 63;
item analysis 63; item banking
64-7; marking schemes 59;
moderation 62; multiple choice
questions 25, 56; norm-referenced

62; Rasch Method 66; results
histogram 61; short answer
questions 56, 59; Skurnik-Nuttal
Measuremeter 63; test analysis
61; test construction 27, 64, 67;
test marking 57-60
timetabling 74-5
training: aims 13; assessment 14;
computing provision 87
transferability: packages 94, 104;
programs 92, 94, 103
tutorial CAL 22

United Kingdom 100

video 38, 44

West Germany 100

Printed in Great Britain
by Amazon

87697521R00075